——SHEWEY'S——

GUIDE AND MAP

—TO THE—

HAPPY HUNTING GROUNDS

—OF—

MISSOURI AND ARKANSAS.

The Paradise of the Hunter and Fisherman.

ARISTA C. SHEWEY,

MAP PUBLISHER,

AND DEALER IN ALL KINDS OF MAPS,

714 PINE STREET,   **ST. LOUIS, MO.**

Fishing ❋ and ❋ Hunting.

200 485 355 7

SOLID
THROUGH TRAINS DAILY.

FROM ST. LOUIS, TO

Kansas City, St. Joseph, Denver St. Paul and Minneapolis.

THE BEST LINE FROM

St. Louis to Cheyenn' and the Black Hills.

Only One Change of Cars from St. Louis to the Pacific Coast,

VIA

DENVER OR ST. PAUL.

TICKET OFFICES:

218 N. Broadway AND Union Depot.

POCKET STATE MAPS.

"CRAM'S"

SHOWS THE RAILWAY SYSTEM IN COLORS.

Printed on BOND PAPER, and will not break and become useless after being folded a few times.

Alabama	$0.25	North Dakota	.25
Alaska, 26x36 inches	1.00	Ohio	.25
Arizona	.25	Oregon	.25
Arkansas	.25	Nova Scotia	.25
British Columbia	.25	Ontario	.25
California	.25	Pennsylvania	.25
Colorado	.25	Quebec	.25
Connecticut	.25	Rhode Island	.25
Delaware	.25	South Carolina	.25
Florida	.25	South Dakota	.25
Georgia	.25	Tennessee	.25
Idaho	.25	Texas	.25
Illinois	.25	United States, Blanchard	.30
Indiana	.25	United States, Cram's	.25
Indian Territory	.25	United States, Official	.50
Iowa	.25	Utah	.25
Louisiana	.25	Vermont	.25
Nevada	.25	Virginia	.25
New Hampshire	.25	Washington	.25
New Jersey	.25	West Virginia	.25
New Mexico	.25	Wisconsin	.25
New York	.25	Wyoming	.25
North Carolina	.25		

STATE MAPS—The above Map, 18x22 inches, mounted on **binder's board.** For handy reference about the desk. Price each, 50 cents.

JOHNSON'S CLASSICAL AND SCRIPTURAL GEOGRAPHY.

WITH NAMES.

Size, 42x50 inches. Price per Map, $5.00.

Oribus, Veteribus, Italia Antiqua, Asia Minor, Orbis Romanus, Cæsar de Bello Gallico, Tavels in St. Paul Outline Map bordering on the Mediterranean, Canaan and Palestine Bible Countries.

HANDY ✣ DESK ✣ MAPS

OF EACH STATE,

MOUNTED ON TARBOARD

——FOR——

OFFICE USE AND FOR SHIPPERS

Are very durable, and will stand any amount of handling
and abuse, and are for quick use.

THE **Railway Systems** are in SEPARATE COLORS, each
color representing a System, making it much more easily to tarce a line, see the Junction points and connec-
tions than on the old style maps.   On each map is a Special
Index to find any railroad however small and remote,
instantly.

An index accompanies each map, giving every town,
village, hamlet and cross roads, with the population, Express, Telegraph, Money Order offices, Banking towns, etc.

Price, single map, on board,   - $ .60
  "   two maps, on board,   - -   1.00

SIZE OF MAPS, 18 x 24 INCHES.

The following named states we can give twice the size,
24x86 inches, and can put any two of the 18x24 inch maps
on the back:

N. Y., Pa., Va, Ill., Tex., Ky. and Tenn.

Price, for three maps,   - $1.50
  "   for one large single map, on board,   .85

These large maps can be hinged to fold the size of the
18x24 inch maps for *15 cents additional*.

ARISTA C. SHEWEY,

MAP PUBLISHER,

AND DEALER IN ALL KINDS OF
MAPS AND ATLASES.   CHICAGO OFFICE, 415 DEARBORN ST.
ST. LOUIS OFFICE, 714 PINE ST.

SHEWEY'S
GUIDE & MAP

——TO THE——

Hunting and
Fishing Grounds

OF MISSOURI and ARKANSAS.

The Paradise of the Hunter and Fisherman

——WITH THE——

Game Laws of every State and Territory in
the United States, British Columbia
and the Provinces, with Maps of
Missouri and Arkansas.

ARISTA C. SHEWEY,
MAP PUBLISHER,

AND DEALER IN ALL KINDS OF MAPS.

714 PINE STREET,   ST. LOUIS, MO.

TABLE OF CONTENTS.

MISSOURI AND ARKANSAS,

THE PARADISE OF THE

HUNTER AND FISHERMAN.

As the season approaches when the lover of the gun and rod anxiously consults the calendar which will once more legitimize this favorite sport, he asks himself with perplexity: Where shall I go this year? Where can I find a place which will fit my time, my pocket and my inclination?

To enable either the deciple of Nimrod or Sir Isaac Walton to choose a place where he can regale himself with the pleasure of hunting and fishing to his heart's delight, we have completed accurate information as to the different resorts in Missouri and Arkansas, where good hotel and camping accommodations can be found with the character of the game and fish incident to such locality and means of reaching the same from St. Louis.

MISSOURI is still furnishing a very large proportion of the game for the markets of all the larger cities of the United States. From October 15th to February 21st of every year, there is not an express car arriving in St. Louis which does not bring large consignments of game. Deer are numerous in the thinly settled mountainous districts, and also in the swampy districts of the southeastern part of the State. These lands and the Ozark mountains consititute the great deer park and game preserve. Game in the Ozarks, of all kinds, is most plentiful. It is joy to the Sportsman on arriving in this country to see the skins of deer and wild cats, foxes and minks, hanging on the posts in front of country stores, while the skins of bears and wolves are not infrequent. Small game is so plentiful that it is practically ignored by the natives.

AN ACT TO PROHIBIT THE EXPORTATION OF GAME AND FISH OUT OF THE STATE OF MISSOURI.

If any agent or servant of any railroad company, express company, steamboat or other common carrier, or private individual, have or receive for transportation or carriage, or for any other purpose, any of the birds or game hereinbefore mentioned, during the season when the cat hing, killing or injuring the same is prohibited, every such person shall be deemed guilty of a misdemeanor.

REVISED STATUTES OF 1889.

ARKANSAS is heavily covered with woodlands, where not only the larger game, such as bear, deer and wild hog, but turkeys, ducks, grouse and quail are denizens, and the streams abound with salmon, black bass and croppie.

AN ACT TO PROHIBIT THE EXPORTATION OF GAME AND FISH OUT OF THE STATE OF ARKANSAS

Section 1. That all the game and fish, except fish in private ponds found within the limits of this State, be, and the same is hereby declared to be, the property of this State; and the hunting, killing and catching of the same is declared to be a privilege.

Section 2. It shall be unlawful for any person to export any fish or game from this State until April 12, 1895; and any person violating the provisions of this Act shall be guil y of a misdeme nor and shall b ; fined, upon convi ;tio i, in any sum not le ;s than twenty-five dollars and no ; more than fifty dollars

Section 3. It shall be unlawful for any Railroad Company, Steamboat, Express Company or any other common carrier to take for carriage any fish or gam ; consigned to points beyond the limits of this State.

Section 4. Any such common carrier may refuse to receive any package which it may suppose contains fish or game desired for export, and may cause said p ickages to be opened, or may sati-fy themselves in any other way that said package does not contain game or fish.

Section 5. Any common carrier violating the provisions of this Act sh ill be deemed guilty of a misdemeanor, and upon con. viction shall be fined in any sum not less than fifty nor more than two hundred dollars.

Section 6. Any violation of this Act shall be prosecuted in the name of the State of Arkansas, and one-half of the fine shall be paid into the County Treasury as other fines are requirhd to be paid, and the other half shall go to the informer.

Section 7. Justices of the Peace shall have jurisdi tion of prosecut ons under this Act.

Section 8. All laws and parts of laws in confli t herewith are hereby repealed and this Act shall be in force from and after its passage.

Approved, April 12, 1889.

AMENDMENT.

Provi e l that it shall not be unl wful under this Act to export b aver opossums, hares or rabbits ground hogs or wood chucks, rac oons squirrels, snipes or plover, provided the same shall te sh pped openly.

Approved, March 31, 1891.

HUNTING AND FISHING POINTS

· · · ON THE · · ·

IRON MOUNTAIN ROUTE.

Mill Creek, Williamsville, Keeners and Poplar Bluff are stations on the Iron Monutain Route in Southeast Missouri, and are also located on the banks of the Black River, which abounds in all kinds of game fish, and is every year visited by hundreds of anglers from a distance. West of these points, and a little more in the interior of Ozark Mountains, is a rapid mountain stream, the Current River. Here is found some of the finest trout fishing in all these regions. By a short land tour this river may be reached from any of the above points, or by rail from Williamsville. At Neeley-ville, itself a very good hunting and fishing point, a branch of the Iron Mountain extends to Doniphan. This point is situated on the banks of the Current River. It is the cen-tre of the great game region of Southeast Missouri, and, in addition to the larger game a hunter is sure to bag tur-keys, partridges, quail, squirrels, etc., which abound in

great quantities. The Belmont branch of the Iron Mountain
Route extends from Bismarck, Mo., to Columbus, Ky.,
passing through very desirable hunting ground, as does
also the Cairo Branch, extending from Cairo to Poplar
Bluff. If it is thought desirable to penetrate far from the
railroad, a good method is to hire a freighter's wagon and
driver who can cook. Plain food is cheap here, and a supply should be taken to last as long as the hunter desires to
stay. From $2.00 to $2.75 per day will pay for the driver
and his rig. Country hotel rates are $1.00 per day, or from
$4.00 to $6.00 per week.

STATIONS IN ARKANSAS.

Corning is the first noted hunting and fishing point
in the State, and is known as the "Sportsmen's Retreat."
"Deer Range," near the town, abounds in deer (as its name
implies), turkeys, ducks, squirrels and all the smaller
game. Corning Lake and the famous Black River are well
stocked with croppie, perch, bass and pickerel. Boats can
be obtained, and huts have been erected along the river,
which are rented at a small cost to hunting parties.

Knobel has good hotel accommodations, game, deer,
turkey, ducks, squirrel, etc. Black bass, jack salmon, croppie, perch, etc., are caught in Mill Lake, Maiden Lake,
Allen Lake, Black and Cache Rivers.

Walnut Ridge is the next good point below Knobel.
Hotel accommodation, all kinds of game from deer down,
in the Black and Cache River bottoms, and on the borders
of the numerous lakes, in which are found, in large quantities, bass, perch, croppie, trout, buffalo and cat fish. Finest sporting grounds in the State. All the varieties of fish
of Northern Arkansas are found in the Cache River and
numerous lakes in the vicinity.

St. Francis River.—This River, flowing through
Eastern Arkansas and emptying into the Mississippi above
Helena, is the most famous duck-hunting resort in the

United States. Flocks of ducks, brant, geese, swan and smaller water fowl swarm the river and its backwaters, from Big Lake to its mouth, throughout the winter season. This river is accessible from Wynne, Earle and other points on the Memphis Extension, and from Forrest City and Marianna on the Helena Branch.

Swifton, farther south, has a large tract of thinly settled country, both to the east and west, that abounds in bear, deer, wolves, wild cats and all small game. Cat and buffalo fish, trout, bass, croppie, white and sun perch, are found in large quantities in Black, White, Cache and Strawberry Rivers, Hollingshead and Clear Lakes.

Newport is a large town, with good hotels and excellent hunting in the vicinity. All kinds of game, such as bear, deer, quail, teal, wood duck and mallards are very plentiful in season. Fish, such as black bass, croppie, jack salmon, channel cat, etc., are found in great quantities.

Batesville is west of Newport, on the White River Branch. It is a large town in a new and mountainous country, abounding in all kinds of game and fish. White River, Polk Bayo, Spring and Miller's Creeks and Spring Creek Lake, team with cat fish, goggle-eyed perch, trout, pike, striped bass, black bass, croppie, salmon, white perch, sturgeon, buffalo and drum fish. Hunting unsurpassed. Good hotels.

A letter from Samuel Cronin, Traveling Freight and Passenger Agent of the H. C. A. & N. Railway, Alexander Division, which is a branch of the Iron Mountain System, and which was opened for business January 1st, says that this country is surely a sportsman's paradise. Deer are plenty and fish in abundance. Trout (they look like our bass) and perch can be easily caught in any of the little and apparently insignificant streams between the Ouachita and Red Rivers. The country is very sparsely settled and hunters should carry their supplies along, such as camp equipage, etc. The country is one vast forest of pine, oak and cypress, principally pine, between the above mentioned rivers.

Hunters' Rates and Special Cars.

Special rates found below have been made via the Iron Mountain Route to hunting parties of three or more. Tickets are good for thirty days, but not later than March 1st, in Missouri, and May 1st, in Arkansas, with stop overs at pleasure, and 150 pounds of baggage, including guns and dogs, will be carried free of charge. Hunting cars, having sleeping accommodations for about thirty, with cook, cooking utensils, dishes and full equipment, may be chartered by parties, and will be side-tracked at any point desired.

For further information, call on or address any of the Company's agents

	FROM ST. LOUIS.	FROM CAIRO.	FROM MEMRHIS.
Augusta	$12 90	$8 40	$4 10
Beebe	12 50	9 20	5 55
Charleston	7 10	1 00	......
Corning	7 70	4 40	5 25
Crawfordsville	12 40	8 35	1 60
Gainesville	8 45	4 65	4 40
Harrisburg	10 25	6 15	3 40
Hoxie	9 05	5 75	......
Knobel	7 90	4 65	5 00
Leeleyville	7 25	8 95	5 70
Nettleton	9 50	5 90	3 40
Newport	10 50	7 20	......
Paragould	8 80	4 65	4 15
Poplar Bluff	6 05	3 35	6 30
Swifton	9 75	6 45	......
Wynne	11 20	7 10	2 80

VALUABLE ASSISTANCE,

The followi- g Traveling and Passenger Agents of the **MISSOURI PACIFIC RAILWAY and IRON MOUNTAIN ROUTE** are constantly looking after the interests of the Line, and will call upon parties comtemplating a trip, and cheerfully furnish them lowest rates of Fare, Maps, Guides. Land Pamphlets, Time Tables, etc. Or they may be addres=ed as follows.

ATCHISON, KAN.
C. E. STYLES ....Passenger and Ticket Agent
AUSTIN, TEX.
J. C. LEWIs ....Traveling Passenger Agent
BOSTON, MASS.
G. K. DELAHANTY. New England Pass'r Agt., 300 Washington St
CAIRO, ILL.
J. W. MASON.... .. ..Passenger Agent
CHATTANOOGA, TENN.
A A. GALLAGHE (.. Southern Passenger Agent, 1.3 Read House
CHICAGO, ILL.
JOHN E. ENNIS...... Dis rict Pass'r and Land Agt., 199 S. Clark St
CINCINNATI, OHIO.
N. R. WARWICK ....District Passenger Agent, 131 Vine St
DENVER, COL.
C. A. TRIPP .. ...General Western Freight and Passenger Agent
INDIANAPOLIS, IND.
COKE ALEXANDER........District Pass'r Agent, 7 Jackson Place
JACKSON, MICH.
H. D. ARMSTRONG ....Traveling Passenger Agent
KANSAS CITY, MO.
E. S. JEWETT........ ....Passenger and Ticket Agent 533 Main St
J. H. LYON ....Western Passenger Agent, 533 Main St
LEAVENWORTH, KAN.
J. N. JOERGER ....Passenger and Ticket Agent
LINCOLN, NEB.
R. P. R, MILLAR..... ....General Agent
LITTLE ROCK, ARK.
H. F. BERKLEY ....Passenger and Ticket Agent
LOUISVILLE, KY.
L. E. DRAKE..... ....Southern Traveling Agent, 319½ 4th St
MEMPHIS, TENN.
H. D. WILSON . ...Passenger and Ticket Agent, 309 Main St
NEW YORK CITY.
W. E HOYT...... General Eastern Passenger Agent, 391 Broadway
J. P. McCANN ... .Eastern Traveling Agent, 391 Broadway
OMAHA, NEB.
J. O. PHILLIPPI.. ...Ass't General Freight and Passenger Agent
THO . F. GODFREY, Pass'r & Tkt Agt., N. E.cor. 13th & Farham Sts
PITTSBURGH, PA.
H. THOMPSON.............Central Passenger Agent 1119 Liberty St
ST.JOSEPH, MO.
F. P. WADE ....Passenger and Ticket Agent
ST. LOUIS, MO.
B. D. CALDWELL.......Ass't General Passenger and Ticket Agent
S. W. ELLIOTT......................City Ticket Agent, 102 N. Fourth St
M. GRIFFIN......................City Passenger Agent, 102 N. Fourth St
W. H. MORTON............. ....Passenger Agent, Union Depot
WICHITA, KAN.
E. E. BLECKLEY... Passenger and Tick t Agent, 120 N. Main St

S. H. H. CLARK,   **H. C. TOWNSEND,**
   1ST VICE-PRES'T & GEN'L MGR.   GEN'L PASS'R & TKT. AGT.
ST. LOUIS, MO.

HUNTING AND FISHING

ON THE

COTTON BELT ROUTE.

The Cotton Belt Route opens up this country, and makes what was formerly an impossible journey to the average man, a trifling matter of ten or twelve hours in a luxurious Pullman.

Leaving St. Louis 7:55 a. m., the first hunting points of any importance are Ardeola and Idalia, 166 and 177 miles from St. Louis, respectively. Here, within a few miles of the stations, deer and turkey are plentiful—not to mention the smaller game, which, in this region, is almost left to the small boy with his irrepressible muzzle-loader.

Guides and teams, at a cost of from $2.00 to $3.00 per day for man and team, can be secured on application to the railroad agent.

Dexter, the next point, 185 miles from St. Louis, is situated in the midst of a beautiful track of prairie land, dotted here and there with islands of trees of from one to fifteen acres in extent. Here is the paradise of the quail and chicken hunter. Two miles in any direction from the station will start covey after covey, while at a distance of ten miles deer can be secured.

No guides are necessary, and teams and dogs can be procured in the town, which also provides good hotel accommodation at $1.50 per day.

Malden, Mo., 202 miles from St. Louis, and 58 miles from Cairo, is the next point, thirty miles south from which, in the vicinity of Big Lake, the ideal of the sportsman is found. No clearing attests the domicile of man; the settler's axe is as yet unheard. The silence of the night is broken only by the solemn hooting of the owl or the blood-curdling screech of the panther. Bears hide in the thicket, and the graceful deer leap the fallen trees in the wild abandon of their freedom. Wildcat, foxes, mink and wild hog are found, and turkey and smaller game are plentiful, while the lake and bayou swarm with flocks of duck, swan, geese, brant and other water-fowl.

Guides and teams can be secured at Malden, and hotel accommodations can be had at that point for $1.00 per day and upwards.

At St. Francis, 213 miles from St. Louis and 70 miles from Cairo, the St. Francis river is crossed. This river abounds in black bass, jack salmon, croppie, perch, etc., and furnishes good duck shooting, while at a distance of 10 or 12 miles deer, turkey, etc., can be found. Guides and teams can be secured on application to the railroad agent.

At Paragould, Ark., 248 miles from St. Louis and 103 miles from Cairo, a branch railroad runs out to St. Francis Lake, 10 miles distant. This lake furnishes excellent fishing, and duck, geese and brant cover its surface, while on Buffalo Island, across the lake, all kinds of game, including bear, deer and turkey, can be found. No guides or teams are necessary, as the Buffalo Island Railroad runs directly to the shores of the lake.

Between Paragould and Jonesboro, the land is covered with timber, and at various distances of from one to ten miles on both sides of the railroad are bayous, furnishing excellent duck shooting, while in the intervening woods deer and turkey are found.

To go south of Jonesboro, it will be necessary to take the Cotton Belt night express, leaving St. Louis 8:20 p. m., and the principal points are Weiner. Fisher and Bemis. The surrounding country partakes of the same general characteristics as that described between Paragould and Jonesboro. The only abodes of man being an occasional saw-mill in the vicinity of the railroad.

At a distance of one mile from Bemis is Crooked Bayou. Fishing is excellent; duck, geese and water fowl in great numbers, and bear, deer, turkey and small game plentiful.

Teams and guides can be hired on application to the railroad agents.

At Clarendon, 330 miles from St. Louis and 215 miles from Cairo, is the White River, in which fish of various kinds, principally trout, bass and croppie, can be found. Duck, geese and other water fowl are plentiful, while the banks and bottom lands both east and west of the railroad furnish bear, deer and smaller game.

South of Clarendon commences the Grand Prairie of Arkansas. which can be reached from Roe, Ulm or Stuttgart. This prairie, 20 miles in width and 80 miles in length, dotted with islands of timber, provides the finest chicken and quail shooting in the West, while the bayous and bottom lands of the White and Arkansas Rivers, which bound the prairie on the north and south, are full of deer and turkey. Teams, etc., can be hired at Ulm or Stuttgart.

Between Cairo and Malden are what is known as the sunk lands, vast marshy tracks, with ridges of dry lands, swarming with duck, geese, swan, brant and all varieties of water fowl. These lands can be reached from LaForge, Ristine, Paw Paw Junction or New Madrid. Good hotel accommodation can be had at New Madrid, also guides and boats.

The various sections of the country south of Malden partaking of the same general characteristics, it is hard to particularize any special spot as either the best or the most desirable, and as the localities which at one time during the season may abound in game, at other times may not be so well stocked, the best plan to pursue would be to purchase tickets to the farthest point which time and means will justify, and stop off at the intermediate points en route until a satisfactory location is found. This can easily be done, as Cotton Belt Hunters' tickets provide for stop-off at pleasure both going and returning.

Below find conditions under which Hunters' tickets are sold ; also round-trip rates from St. Louis and Cairo.

Hunters' tickets will be sold to parties of three or more on one ticket, commencing Octobor 1st, limited to thirty days from the date of sale, but in no case later than March 1st to points in Missouri, or May 1st to points in Arkansas. Stop-over will be permitted to all points within the limit of the ticket, and guns, dogs and camping outfits to the amount of 200 pounds will be carried free for each passenger.

HUNTERS' RATES

To Points on St. Louis, Arkansas & Texas Railway.

TO		FROM CAIRO.	FROM ST. LOUIS OR E. ST. LOUIS.
La Forge..o		$1 70	¢ 8 70
Paw Paw Jc.	''	2 0J	8 7i
Ardeola.	''	....	6 70
Day	''	....	6 9J
Idalia	'	....	7 10
Dex er.	''	....	7 40
Malden		2 85	8 1u
St. Fr ncis ....Ark.		3 3J	8 6i
Para ould	''	4 65	8 75
Joue boro	''	5 50	9 50
Obe r	''	6 05	1U 15
Weiner	''	6 35	10 45
Fisher	''	6 7i	10 85
Tilton	''	7 2J	11 3J
Hunter	''	8 00	12 05
Brinkl y	'	8 4i	12 55
Clarendon	''	9 10	13 20
Roe	''	9 35	13 45
Stuttgart	''	9 35	13 95

If hunting parties will notify any of the following, an Agent of the Company will meet them at St. Louis or Cairo, and render all assistance possible in the way of help and information.

J. E. DAVENPORT,   **S. G. HATCH,**

CITY PASSENGER AND TICKET AGENT.   TRAVELING PASSENGER AGENT.

NO. 215 NORTH FOURTH STREET, ST. LOUIS, MO.

J. H. JONES,   **M. ADAMI,**

TICKET AGENT.   ' TRAVELING PASSENGER AGENT.

CAIRO, ILLINOIS.

D. MILLER,   **E. W. LaBEAUME,**

GENERAL TRAFFIC MANAGER.   GENERAL PASSENGER AGENT

W. B. DODDRIDGE, GENERAL MANAGER.

ST LOUIS, MO.

HUNTING AND FISHING

ON THE

FRISCO LINE.

It is a well known fact to sportsmen that there is no section of the western country that affords better hunting and fishing than Southwestern Missouri, Arkansas, Indian Territory and Southern Kansas, traversed by the Frisco Line. The Meramec River, crossed several times by this Line, affords excellent fishing. The Gasconade and Little Piney Rivers, crossed at Jerome, Mo., by this Line, are noted for their game fish. The James River, near Springfield, Mo., is another fine stream for fishing; the Spring River, near Verona, Mo.; the Grand River, near Seneca, Mo.; the Virdigris River, near Virdigris, I. T.; the White River, near Eureka Springs, Ark.; the Kiamichi River, near Kosoma, I. T., all abound with game fish.

The hunting is good in all the counties of Southwest Missouri and Northwestern Arkansas. Large and small game of all kinds are plentiful, and no mistake can be made by going to the Ozark, Boston and Kiamichi Mountains, on the Frisco Line, for excellent sport.

Enquire of game dealers in St. Louis, and you will learn that the most game and greatest variety come from the Frisco Line.

This Line sells round-trip excursion tickets to parties of three or more on one solid ticket from October 1st to March 31st. Tickets are limited thirty days from date of sale. From St. Louis to, viz.:

Salem, Mo.	$ 5 00	Seneca, Mo.	$13 00
Jerome, Mo.	5 00	Winslow, Ark.	15 00
Crocker, Mo.	5 90	St. Paul, Ark.	15 50
Chadwick, Mo.	11 00	Mansfield, Ark	17 90

For further particulars address nearest Station Agent of the Frisco Line, or D. Wishart, General Passenger Agent, St. Louis, Mo.

HUNTING AND FISHING GROUNDS

ALONG THE

Kansas City, Springfield & Memphis Line

IN SOUTHWESTERN MISSOURI AND ARKANSAS.

The statistics have been carefully gathered by representative sportsmen who reside in that region, and much valuable information about the prospects for game, the kind of game that most abounds, the topography of the country, and the accommodations and facilities offered to sportsmen. The reports generally show an abundance of game, including bear, deer, turkeys, ducks and quail, and also plenty of excellent fishing.

The best turkey and quail shooting is reported from Rogersville to Gilmore, a distance of 140 miles, turkey being so plentiful that the trainmen have no difficulty in bagging all they need for their own use from the track, where they come in flocks during the dry weather to scratch in the gravel along the line of the road. Deer are to be found in large quantities between Norwood and Hatchiecoon, but west of that range are scarcer.

Thayer, Oregon County, Missouri, is one of the first points on the line where game is reported to be plentiful. The hunting grounds in that vicinity extend over an area of about forty miles square, and are known to sportsmen as the celebrated Irish Wilderness and Indian Camp. Deer, turkey, quail and duck are thick, and the season will not close until the latter part of February. Dogs and guides can be secured at reasonable rates by visiting sportsmen, and the hotel accommodations are good and charges low. There being no objection on the part of property owners to hunting on their grounds, this point is one of the best on the line for sport.

At Mammoth Springs in Arkansas, the game is plentiful over a large territory; deer, turkey, quail and squirrel being the principal species, and quail and turkey being most numerous. The season extends over a period of three months, from November to February; guides can be secured at 50 cents per day, board at $1.00 and livery $3.00 per day. There, are few dogs in the vicinity, however, and sportsmen who shoot over dogs exclusively will find it necessary to take their own. There are no objections made to hunters.

The hunting grounds in the neighborhood of Big Bay, in Craighead County, cover a radius of about twenty miles. There are some deer and an abundance of bear. Turkey and duck are plentiful, and the season runs from September to May, while deer are shot as late as February, squirrel are also thick in that region, and hunters are not molested in that territory. Heavy breech-loading guns and Winchesters are suggested as the weapons to be used, and gum boots and rubber coats are necessary to a complete outfit.

Oakdornick is the name of the hunting grounds that are located at about a mile and a half from Hatchiecoon, and is the headquarters of the southern sportsmen, the Chickasaw Gunning and Trolling Club and the Osceola Ducking Club of Memphis, both having club-houses and leased grounds in that vicinity. The duck, turkey and squirrel shooting is excellent during the entire season, which runs from October 15 to February 1, and there is a large lake near the Hatchiecoon, where the duck are very plentiful; it also affords rare sport for the angler. All that is necessary for the visiting sportsman is to get a permit from the secretary of either club, and the privilege is freely accorded.

At Big Creek, a mile or so out of Gilmore, there are plenty of bear, deer, turkey, duck and squirrel, and the fishing is the best in the Southwest. There being no hotels of any consequence in the neighborhood and the country unbroken and very sparsely settled, sportsmen visiting there will find a camp outfit necessary. The season lasts from October 15 to February 1, and the best time to visit that point is during November and December. Last year ducks were killed by the thousands, and they are just as plentiful now. Turkeys are also abundant and quite a number of bear and deer have been shipped out of Gilmore.

The hunting grounds are easily reached from Kansas City, the Fort Scott & Gulf and Springfield & Memphis line running directly through them. Sportsmen can leave this city at 6:30 in the evening and arrive at Thayer for breakfast the following morning, and if they desire to go further south, they reach Hatchiecoon by noon.

Special round-trip rates for hunting parties can be had on application to any ticket agent of the Fort Scott and Gulf line, or to the General Passenger Agent. Tents and Camp Equipage, if in convenient shape for handling and not of unreasonable weight, and carried free in baggage car. For further information address,

J. E. LOCKWOOD,

General Passenger Agent,

KANSAS CITY.

Illinois Hunting and Fishing.

Among the important Hunting and Fishing resorts **Spring Lake,** situated near Manito, on the Jacksonville & Southeastern Railway, cannot be surpassed for its elegant fishing—bass, pickerel, croppie and other game fish are bountiful and afford delightful sport.

Small game can be found in season, thereby affording good hunting. This lake is about 18 miles in length and from 100 yards to ¼-mile in width, and is within a short distance of Copperas Creek dam, located at government lock, "a beautiful resort." Upwards of fifty people can be comfortably accommodated at Spring Lake, and a large club house and hotel will be erected in a short time by the Pekin and Spring Lake Hunting and Fishing Club, which has recently been organized. Capital stock, $50,000.

Quiver Lake is another resort on Illinois River, located near Havana, also affords splendid hunting and fishing. Ample accommodation for all.

Long Lake and Horse-Shoe Lake, well-known resorts, are located on J. S. E. Line. These lakes are only about twelve miles from St. Louis. Fishing is very good, boats, etc., can be obtained at the lakes.

In addition to above mentioned resorts, there are several others located on J. S. E. Line that furnish great sport.

Sport seekers rates the year around to all these places.

Address,

H. A. SUTTLE,

General Passenger Agent,

513 Chestnut St., St. Louis.

HUNTING AND FISHING POINTS

ON THE

Hannibal & St. Joseph Railway.

BURLINGTON ROUTE.

Swan Lake, three and one-half miles south of Wheeling, Mo. Several good lakes on the "bottom" lands below "Swan Lake," equally as good as Swan Lake. Good hotel accommodations are afforded at Wheeling for those desiring to visit this locality.

There are two lakes, one 2½ miles, and the other three miles southwest of Utica, Mo. Good hotel accommodations. A number of timber lakes on the prairie near the same locality are equally good.

The bottom lands one and one-half miles east of Utica, Mo., offers good inducements for duck hunting, as also other game. Good rabbit and quail hunting may be found in the vicinity of Holt, Kearney and Robertson, Mo.

A large lake with a variety of fish, three miles south of Liberty, with first-class facilities for fishing. Good hotel accommodations at Liberty.

Lake Contrary, one mile south of St. Joseph, affords good fishing. A good hotel being situated at the lake, boat houses, etc.

POINTS ON THE

K. C., ST. J. & C. B. R. R.

BURLINGTON ROUTE.

Bean Lake, a point forty miles north of Kansas City, Mo., fine hunting and fishing. New hotel erected for accommodation for the benefit of people who go there to hunt and fish.

From Amazonia to Hopkins on the Hopkins Branch, and to Corning on the Main Line, good hunting and hotel accommodations at the different stations.

Langdon, the hunting and fishing is fine. This place has become quite a resort for the people in the county. Good accommodations can be had at all times.

THE OPEN SEASONS.

The appended synopsis of the game and fish laws of all the States and Territories of the United States, and of the British Provinces.

CAUTION.

The Game.Laws printed herein are corrected up to August 1st, 1891. Owing to frequent changes made at the session of each legislature, we would advise sportsmen and hunters to make inquiry from the State or Territorial officials to learn if any changes have been made.

ALABAMA.—In the counties of Monroe, Clarke, Wilcox, Talladega, Bibb, Autauga, Clay, deer, October 20 to February 14; wild turkeys, October 20 to May 1; turtle doves, August 1 to April 1, and Montgomery County, July 10 to April 1; quails or partridges, September 15 to March 15; ducks, October 1 to May 1. · In Perry County: doves, July 1 to March 15; quails, October 15 to March 15; deer, October 15 to February 15; ducks, October 1 to April 1; turkeys, October 20 to May 1. Mobile and Baldwin counties: deer, November 1 to February 1; turkeys and quails, November 1 to April 1; turtle doves, September 1 to April 1; ducks, November 1 to May 1. Barbour County: deer, October 20 to May 1; quails, September 1 to May 1; turtle doves, August 1 to May 1. Butler and Elmore counties: deer, October 20 to February 15; turkeys, October 20 to May 1; quails, September 15 to March 15; turtle doves, August 1 to April 1. Calhoun and Tuscaloosa counties: deer, turkeys and quails, November 1 to March 1; turtle doves, July 15 to March 1. Chilton and Sumter counties: deer September 15 to February 15; turkeys, September 15 to May 1; turtle doves, August 1 to March 15; quails, October 1 to April 1. Colbert, Covington, Jefferson, Lauderdale, Marengo, Pike and St. Clair counties: deer, September 1 to April 1; turkeys and quails, October 1 to April 1; quails protected in Covington County. Coosa County: deer, October 1 to April 1; turkeys, October 1 to May 1. Cullman, Limestone and Madison counties: deer, July 4 to February 1; turkeys and quails, September 1 to March 1. Dallas County: deer, October 20 to February 4: turkeys, October 20 to April 1; turtle doves, July 10 to April 1; quails, October 10 to March 15. Greene County: deer, November 1 to January 10; turkeys, November 1 to April 15; quails, November 1 to March 1; turtle doves, November 1 to February 1. Hale County: deer, October 1 to February 1; turkeys, October 15 to May 1; quails, March 15 to November 1; turtle doves, July 15 to March 15. Lawrence County: quails, October 15 to March 25. Lowndes County: deer, October 20 to February 14; turkeys, October 20 to April 1; turtle doves, July 4 to April 1; quails, October 10 to March 15. Macon County: deer, October 1 to February 1; turkeys, Octo ber 1 to May 1; turtle doves, July 15 to April 1; quails, October 1 to March 1. Montgomery County: deer, October 2) to February 14; turkeys, October 20 to May 1; turtle doves, July 10 to April 1; quails, October 15 to March 15; ducks, October 1 to May 1. Perry County: deer, October 15 to February 15; protected east of the Cahaba River. Turkeys, October 20 to May 1; turtle doves July 1 to March 15; quails, October 15 'to March 15; ducks, October 1 to April 1. Pickens County: deer, September 15 to February 1; turkeys, September 15 to April 15; turtle doves, August 1 to April 1; quails, October 15 to March 15; ducks, October 1 to April 1. Camp hunting, use of nets, traps and devices other than a shoulder gun, night hunting, floats, sneak boats, box or battery shooting, prohibited in nearly every county. State law forbids Sunday shooting. Birds' nests and eggs protected, except those of birds of prey. Dams, traps, weirs, or other obstructions to the free passage of fish up streams, and poisons, drugs and explosives prohibited

ALASKA.—The erection of dam ', barricades, or other obstructions, in any river, which would prevent fish from reaching their spawning grounds, prohibited.

ARIZONA.—Elks, deer, antelopes, mountain sheep, mountain goats, October 1 to February 1. Partridges, wild turkeys, geese, brants, swans, curlews, plovers, snipes, quails and ducks, September 1 to March 1. Prairie chickens or pinnated grouse protected to 1892 The capture of fish by means of nets or explosives prohibited.

ARKANSAS.—Deer, August 1 to February 1. Turkeys, September 1 to May 1. Prairie chickens, September 1 to February 1. Quails, October 1 to March 1. Netting or snaring of quails, prairie chickens and turkeys prohibited, except on a person's own premises during open season and at any time to protect fruit. Yell County, partridges and quails, September 15 to March 15. Wild turkeys, August 15 to April 15. Nests of all birds protected except those of crows, blackbirds, hawks, owls, eagles and birds of prey. Possession and transportation prohibited during the close season. Exportation of game and fish prohibited until April 12, 1895, except beavers, opossums, hares or rabbits, ground hogs, woodchucks raccoons, squirrels, snipes and plovers, provided the same shall be shipped openly. All fish, except in private ponds, declared to be the property of the State, and catching same a privilege. Netting, seining, trapping, dragging or maintaining any obstructions in the waters of the State prohibited: provided, small seines may be used for catching minnows for bait; and for supplying necessary food. but not for sale, nets having meshes not less than three inches in size may be used in navigable waters.

CALIFORNIA.—Deer, antelopes, elks and mountain sheep protected until 1893. Quails, partridges, grouse of any kind, ducks and rails, October 1 to March 1. Doves, July 1 to January 1. Wild turkeys, Bob White quails, pheasants and skylarks protected until January 1, 1895. Blue and white cranes protected. Netting and snaring of game and insectivorous birds prohibited ; eggs and nests protected. Trout, April 1 to November 1 ; taking of trout, except with hook and line, prohibited. Salmon, October 1 to August 31. Fishing between 6 p. m. Saturday and sundown of succeeding Sunday, prohibited. The pollution of waters with lime, sawdust, drugs or any substance deleterious to fish, and the use of explosives or any poisonous substance, or nets, weirs, traps or similar devices, prohibited. Marketing of shad weighing less than eight pounds prohibited. Permission of owner of premises required in most counties to hunt or fish.

COLORADO.—Deer, elks and antelopes which have horns, July 1 to December 1. Not more than five deer, five antelopes and two elks allowed to be killed in any one year by one person, and hides of same may be shipped out of the State by obtaining a tag for each from the county clerk. The killing for food is limited to the immediate and necessary use of the person killing the animal, game bird or fish. Killing for market or sale prohibited. Hounding prohibited. Exportation of game and fish prohibited. Mountain sheep protected until March 26, 1897. Buffalos and mountain goats protected until March 26, 1899. Prairie chickens, grouse, quails and pheasants, September 1 to November 15. Ducks, brants, geese and swans, September 1 to April 1. Wild turkeys, larks, whip-poor-wills and all other song and insectivorous birds protected. Owner's consent necessary to hunt in any inclosure. Night hunting, netting and trapping prohibited. Trout or any food fish for immediate use, May 1 to December 1. Fishing with hook and line only permitted. The use of explosives, drugs, nets, seines, weirs and the pollution of streams with sawdust or other deleterious substances, prohibited. The State is divided into four game districts, with paid game and fish wardens.

CONNECTICUT.—Quails, woodcocks, ruffed grouse (called partridges), and gray squirrels, October 1 to January 1. Exportation of quails, woodcocks and grouse prohibited. Eggs and nests are protected. Wild ducks. geese and brants, September 1 to May 1. Nests and eggs of above protected equally. Trapping, snaring or netting of woodcocks, quails and ruffed grouse forbidden, except on a man's own grounds. Possession by any person, or any express company, or carrier, during the close season is forbidden. Exportation of game prohibited. Shooting or being with gun and dog without leave on the inclosed grounds of any individual or corporation where notices forbidding hunting are posted is a breach of law even in the open season. Shooting, hunting, or having firearms in possession on Sunday in the open air is illegal. Song and insectivorous birds and their nests protected. Restrictions placed upon certain parts of Housatonic River and flats, hunting being prohibited except on Tuesdays and Fridays between October 20 and April 20. Rails may be shot in New Haven, Fairfield and Litchfield counties from August 20 to January 1; other portions of the State from September 1 to January 1. Rabbits not protected. The use of ferrets for hunting rabbits prohibited. Trout, April 1 to July 1. Unlawful to sell trout less than six inches long. Fishing in any other way than with hook and line, and within four hundred yards of any fishway, prohibited. Black bass, June 11 to May 1. Striped bass or salmon shall not be caught in seines or nets from June 20 to July 13, and striped bass must not weigh less than one-half pound. Shad, March 1 to June 20. Numerous local laws govern fishing ponds and streams. Netting ponds and lakes forbidden. A game and a fish warden in each county is appointed by the county commissioners.

DELAWARE.—Partridges, grouse, quails, rabbits and hares: in New Castle County, November 15 to January 1; in Kent and Sussex counties, November 15 to February 1. Reedbirds, ortolans and rails, September 1 to February 1. Geese, swans, brants and ducks, except Summer or woodducks, October 1 to April 15. Woodcocks, July 1 to September 15 and in New Castle County, November 15 to January 1, and in Kent and Sussex counties, November 15 to February 1. Non-residents must procure a license (fee $25) from the Delaware Game Protective Association. Netting or snaring and night-hunting of partridges, grouse, woodcocks and quails, and trespass, and hunting game birds in snow prohibited. Hunting wildfowl with punt or swivel guns or with light prohibited. Insectivorous birds and their nests (except on one's own premises) protected. Muskrats, December 1 to March 30. Sunday hunting illegal. Shipment of game, except ducks and geese, out of a county or State without license is illegal, unless the shipper make oath that the game was legally killed and is not intended for sale or profit. Residents may ship one dozen or less birds out of the State without a license. Black bass and trout, in New Castle County, June 1 to November 1; less than six inches in length protected.

DISTRICT OF COLUMBIA.—Partridges or quails, November 1 to February 1. Pheasants or ruffed grouse, August 1 to February 1. Woodcocks, July 1 to February 1. Prairie chickens, September 1 to February 1. Snipes and plovers, September 1 to May 1. Geese and ducks, September 1 to April 1. Reed birds and ortolans, September 1 to February 1. Deer, August 15 to January 1. Insectivorous birds protected, also nests and eggs. Trap or snare and swivel gun, Sunday shooting, night shooting, and trespass, prohibited. Fishing with hook and line, at any time.

FLÓRIDA.—Deer may be killed, in each county, for four months of the year, said four months to be designated by the respective county ommissioners, whose duty it is to publish same in some local newspa- or post it. Quails, partridges and turkeys, November 1 to March 1 Fire hunting, snaring and trapping prohibited

GEORGIA.—Richmond County, deer, October 1 to January 1. Fawns protected. Wild turkeys and partridges (quails), October 15 to April 1. Summer ducks and doves, July 1 to April 1. Woodcocks, August 15 to January 1. Trapping and netting, poisoning, and destruction of nests of any game or insectivorous birds, prohibited. Dougherty, Randolph, Calhoun and Baker counties, deer and partridges (quails), October 1 to April 1. Lincoln and Baldwin counties, does and fawns, August 1 to Jan. uary 1; bucks, May 1 to September 1, and November 1 to March 1. Wild turkeys and partridges (quails), October 15 to March 15. Clarke, Fulton, Camden, Bartow, Floyd, Chatham and Whitfield counties, deer, partridges (quails), wild turkeys, doves and wild ducks, October 1 to April 1, except Fulton County, where doves may be killed from August 1 to April 1. Many other county laws Fire-hunting deer within the State prohibited, except on one's own premises, or with full consent of the owner of the lands hunted on. Sunday shooting prohibited. Fishing with hook and line permitted; traps, nets, weirs, etc., drugs, explosives, obstructions, etc., prohibited.

IDAHO.—Buffalos, elks, deer, antelopes and mountain sheep, September 1 to January 1. Moose protected until 1897. Sage hens, pheasants, grouse and prairie chickens, July 15 to February 1. Geese and ducks, August 1 to April 15. Netting of fish prohibited except in taking salmon and sturgeon. No close season on fish.

ILLINOIS.—Deer and turkeys, September 1 to January 15. Pinnated grouse or prairie chickens, September 15 to November 1. Ruffed grouse or quails, October 1 to December 1. Partridges or pheasants and quails, October 1 to December 1. Woodcocks, July 15 to September 15. Geese, brant ducks, or other waterfowl, September 15 to April 15. Gray, red, fox or black squirrels, June 1 to December 15. Possession and sale of game prohibited in close season, except game brought in from other States, which may be sold from October 1 to February 1. The sale or exportation of quails, grouse, squirrels and turkeys killed within the State, prohibited. Doves and insectivorous birds and their nests protected. Bounty of two cents per head paid on English sparrows. Trapping, night hunting, swivel guns, shooting from sink boat, sailboat or steamboat, and artificial blinds prohibited. Hunting or fishing within the enclosures of others without leave is a punishable misdemeanor. Obstructions in or across any stream so as to obstruct the free passage of fish up, down or through such watercourse prohibited; the law prohibits the taking of fish with any device other than hook and line, except minnows for bait, within one-half mile of any dam; prohibits the use of spears, acids medical and chemical compounds or explosives; prohibits fishing through the ice from December 1 to March 1. Three game wardens, to be appointed by the Governor.

INDIANA.—Deer, October 1 to January 1; chasing or worrying at any time and trapping prohibited. Quails and pheasants (ruffed grouse), October 15 to December 20. Wild turkeys, November 1 to February 1. Prairie chickens, September 1 to February 1. Woodcocks, July 1 to January 1. Wild ducks, September 1 to April 15. Squirrels, June 1 to December 20. Wild pigeons protected from any kind of molestation within a half mile of nesting. Insectivorous and song birds, their nests and eggs, except English sparrows, crows, hawks and other birds of prey, protected. Hunting with dogs or shooting on inclosed lands without written permission, forbidden. Any dog found roaming over the country unattended by owner or agent shall be deemed a run-about dog and may be legally killed. Sale, possession and transportation in close season prohibited; and the transportation beyond the State at any time is forbidden. Gigging and spearing fish allowed only from July 1 to January 1. Artificially stocked waters protected for three years after planting fish. Nets, seines, shooting, explosives and poisons prohibited. Hook and line fishing allowed at any time. Road supervisors are constituted officers of the law and are compelled by its provisions to enforce the same.

INDIAN TERRITORY.—The Government prohibits every person, other than an Indian, from hunting or fishing.

IOWA.—Prairie chickens, September 1 to December 1. Woodcocks July 10 to January 1. Ruffed grouse or pheasants, quails and wild turkeys, October 1 to January 1. Deer and elks, September 1 to January 1. Any wild duck, goose or brant, August 15 to May 1. Not more than twenty-five each of grouse, woodcocks or quails to be killed in any one day by any one person. Beavers, minks, otters and muskrats, November 1 to April 1 (for the protection of private property at any time). Trapping, snaring and netting of above birds forbidden. The killing of pinnated grouse, woodcocks, quails or ruffed grouse, for traffic, declared unlawful; and shipping or carrying them out of the State is forbidden. Not to exceed one dozen per day may be shipped to any person within the State. Use of swivel gun or poison prohibited. Bass, wall-eyed pike and cropples, May 15 to November 1. Salmon and trout, · April 1 to November 1. Traps, nets, seines, trot lines, spears an obstructions of any kind, explosives and poisonous drugs, prohibited. Transportation or sale during close season prohibited. Trespass and fishing in stocked waters forbidden. Hook and line fishing only permitted, except that a net not exceeding five yards in length may be used to catch minnows, and buffalo fish and suckers only may be speared between November 1 and March 1.

KANSAS.—Prairie chickens or pinnated grouse, September 1 to January 1. Quails, November 1 to January 1. Snaring and trapping prohibited. Pursuing or hunting game of any kind on improved or occupied land, without consent of owner, prohibited. Unlawful to catch black bass, croppies, or wall-eyed pike except with rod, line and hook. All other fish, May 1 to July 1.

KENTUCKY.--Deer, males not · protected; females September 1 to March 1. Wildfowl, September 15 to May 1. Wild turkeys, September 1 to February 1 Woodcocks, June 1 to January 1. Quails and ruffed grouse, October 1 to March 1. Doves, August 1 to February 1. Song and insectivorous birds, and nests of all birds, protected. Trapping, snaring and netting forbidden.

LOUISIANA.—Deer and ducks, October 1 to March 1. Turkeys, October 1 to April 15. Quails, partridges and pheasants, October 1 to April 1. Insectivorous birds protected. Nests and eggs protected. In the parish of Orleans, woodducks, July 1 to October 1. Deer, August 1 to March 1. Rabbits and hares, May 1 to August 1. Quails, October 1 to April 1. Night herons, July 1 to October 1. Marsh hens, May 1 to August 1. Song birds protected, except grasses, larks, caille doves martins, papabottes and swallows. This is the general State law The police juries of the different parishes have the right to regulate the season in regard to deer, ducks, turkeys, quails, partridges and pheasants, and in many parishes they have done so. Where the police juries do not regulate the time for their respective parishes, the general State law governs. Nets, seines, traps, weirs, etc., poisons, drugs, pollution of streams, or any obstruction to the free passage of fish, prohibited.

MAINE.—Moose, deer and caribou, October 1 to January 1. Deer, on the Island of Mt. Desert, November 1 to January 1. The killing or having in possession, except alive, of more than one moose, two caribous and three deer is prohibited. Hounding illegal. Any person may lawfully kill any dog found hunting moose, deer or caribou. Minks, beavers, sables, otters, fishers and muskrats, October 15 to May 1. Woodducks, dusky ducks (black ducks), teals and gray ducks, September 1 to April 1. Ruffed grouse (partridge) and woodcocks, September 1 to December 1. Quails, October 1 to December 1. Pinnated grouse (prairie chickens), September 1 to January 1. Plovers, August 1 to May 1. Trapping, netting, snaring and killing any wild duck or game bird otherwise than with a shoulder gun prohibited. Insectivorous birds and their nests protected, excepting crows, English sparrows, hawks and owls. The Governor may commission persons to take birds or nests for scientific purposes, but the whole number holding commissions shall not exceed ten at any one time. A bounty of five dollars paid for every wolf and bear killed in any town. Transportation and exportation of game prohibited, unless tagged and open to view. Shooting and hunting on Sunday prohibited. Black bass, July 1 to April 1; illegal to take at any time from their spawning beds. No salmon, shad or other migratory fish shall be taken or fished for within five hundred yards of any fishway, dam or millrace, nor in the Penobscot River between the mouth of the Kenduskeag Stream and the waterworks dam at Treat's Falls, on said river; nor between the Augusta highway bridge over the Kennebec River and the Augusta dam, between April 1 and November 1, except with a single hook and line, nor shall hook and line or artificial flies be used at any time within one hundred yards of any fishway, dam or millrace; provided that fly fishing shall be allowed up to the bridge across Denny's River at Lincoln's Mill, but not between the said bridge and Lincoln's milldam. No salmon shall be killed or taken in any manner between July 15 and April 1, except that between July 15 and September 15 salmon may be taken with a rod and single line. Alewives, April 1 to July 15; not allowed to be taken at any time in non-tidal or non-navigable waters by any net other than the ordinary hand dipnet. Smelts, in tidal waters, with hook and line only, October 1 to April 1. Land-locked salmon, trout and togue, May 1 to October 1, except on the St. Croix River and its tributaries, and all the waters in Kennebec County, which is from May 1 to September 15. White perch, July 1 to April 1. During February, March and April *bona fide* citizens of Maine may fish for and take to their own homes land-locked salmon, trout and togue. Grapnels, spears, trawls, weirs, nets, scenes, traps, spoons, setlines, or any device other than the single baited hook and line, or with artificial flies, prohibited in all fresh water lakes, ponds and streams The taking of sea salmon or land-locked salmon less than nine inches in length, or trout less than five inches in length, prohibited. Not more than fifty pounds, at any one time, of land-locked salmon, trout or togue, in all, allowed to be transported by one person, and must be in possession of the owner. Dip-nets, with meshes smaller than one inch square in the clear, in any waters frequented by migratory fishes except the St. Croix River, October 1 to April 1. The pollution of streams by offal of any kind prohibited. Special laws govern the sea and shell fish industries ..... Special laws: Trout, land-locked salmon or other fish in the Misery and Saccatien or Socatian rivers which empty into Moosehead Lake, may be taken only from May 1 to September 10 ...... Trout and land-locked salmon in the Kennebag), Rangeley, Cupsuptic, Mooselucmaguntic, Mollychunkamunk and Welokeunebacook Lakes, or in streams flowing into or connecting said lakes, may be taken nly from May 1 to February 1. The use of spawn as bait for fishing in any of the foregoing

waters during September prohibited......Trout or   nd-locked salmon
in the Rangeley Stream between the mouth of the Kennebago Stream
and the head of the island at the eddy, so-called; and in the South Bog
Stream which empties into Rangeley Lake, above the dead water at the
mouth of said stream; and in the Bemis Stream which empties into
Mooselucmaguntic Lake, above the blue water, at the mouth of said
stream; and in the Cupsuptic Stream which empties into CupsupticLake,
between the first falls toward its mouth and its source, May 1 to July 1.
Kennebago Stream between the foot of the first falls toward its mouth
and the upper falls at the outlet of Kennebago Lake, May 1 to September
1. That portion of Rangeley Stream from the head of the island at the
eddy to the Rangeley Dam is protected at all times. Fish may be taken
only from May 1 to October 1 in the following ponds: Blue Mountain,
Tufts, Grindstone, Dutton, Beaver, Long Potter's and Four Ponds. Togue
protected in Anonymous Pond until 1895. Trout protected in Chase's
Pond until 1894. Trout and pickerel protected in Great, Shorey's, Sta-
ples' and Parker's brooks until 1893. Kneeland Pond fish protected until
1893. Pickerel may be taken with hook and line in Little Sebago Pond
June 1 to October 1. Fish protected in Long and Weeks' Ponds and
Woodsum's Brook until 1894. Nevers', Carsley, Rogers', Tingley and
Lakin brooks protected until 1895. Perkins' and Nute brooks protected
until 1892.

MARYLAND.—Woodcocks, State law, June 15 to February 1. County
laws: Anne Arundel, Caroline, Kent, Prince Georges, Queen Anne, July
4 to February 1 ; Carroll, Montgomery, July 1 to January 1 ; Charles,
Cecil, July 4 to February 4 ; Harford, June 10 to January 1 ; Talbot,
July 4 to January 1 ; Wicomico, June 15 to February 1 ; Howard, June 15
to December 24. Rabbits, State law, October 15 to January 15. County
laws: Allegheny, September 1 to January 1 ; Frederick, October 15 to
January 1 ; Montgomery, September 1 to February 1 ; Cecil, Harford,
November 1 to January 10 ; Worcester, November 1 to January 15 ; Baltimore, November 1 to December 26 ; Dorchester, October 20 to February
1 : Howard, October 24 to December 24 ; Carroll, October 1 to December
24 ; Garrett, September 1 to December 1 : Washington, August 12 to January 1. Wild turkeys, county laws: Frederick, November 15 to January 15 ; Garrett; September 15 to January 1. Quails or partridges, State
law, November 1 to December 24. County laws: Allegheny, Frederick,
Talbot, October 15 to January 1 ; Queen Anne, October 15 to January 1 ;
Baltimore, October 1 to December 26 ; Caroline, Worcester, Somerset,
November 1 to February 1 ; Howard, October 24 to December 24 ; Cecil,
Harford, November 1 to January 10 ; Carroll, October 20 to December
24 ; Montgomery, November 1 to December 15 ; Dorchester, October 20
to February 1 ; Washington, October 20 to January 1 ; Wicomico, November 1 to January 1. Pheasants, Cecil, September 5 to February 1 ; Harford, September 1 to February 1 ; Howard, August 15 to December 24.

Rail and reed birds: Cecil, September 5 to February 1 ; Harford, September 1 to February 1 ; Talbot, September 10 to January 1   Squirrels, county laws: Carroll, September 1 to December 24 ; Wicomico, September 1 to February 15.   Plovers and sandpipers, county laws: Wicomico, November 1 to January 1.   Wood and Summer ducks, county laws: Talbot and Wicomico, September 10 to January 1.   Minks, otters and muskrats, Wicomico County, December 15 to March 15.   Deer, October 1 to January 1.   Hounding prohibited.   Speckled brook trout and speckled river trout, April 1 to August 15.   Hook and line fishing only allowed. Sunday fishing for trout prohibited.   Use of swivel or big guns, and night shooting, prohibited.   License necessary in Caroline, Charles, Dorchester, Howard, Anne Arundel and Baltimore counties.   In all above counties except Caroline written permission from landowner is required in lieu of license and in Garrett County is absolutely necessary.   Exportation of game is forbidden from Montgomery, Worcester, Wicomico and Caroline counties.   Many insectivorous birds are protected in Montgomery County.

MASSACHUSETTS.—Deer protected. Gray squirrels, hares and rabbits, September 1 to March 1. Ruffed grouse or partridges and woodcocks, September 15 to January 1. Quails, October 15 to January 1. Prairie chickens or pinnated grouse protected. Ducks, all kinds, September 1 to April 15. Plovers, snipes, rails, sandpipers and other shore, marsh and beach birds, July 15 to May 1. Wild and passenger pigeons, gulls and terns, October 1 to May 1. Shooting at wildfowl and shore birds prohibited in the harbor and great ponds of Nantucket and the waters in and around the islands of Tuckernuck, Muskeget and the Gravelly Islands. All wild and insectivorous birds not named above, except English sparrows, crow blackbirds, crows, jays, birds of prey and wild geese, protected. Snaring, trapping, use of ferrets, battery, swivel or pivot guns, and torch or other artificial light prohibited. Black bass, July 1 to December 1. Trout, lake trout and land-locked salmon, April 1 to September 1; trout, in Berkshire, Hampshire and Franklin counties, April 1 to August 1. Hampden, April 1 to September 1. Salmon, May 1 to August 1. Smelts, June 1 to March 15. Black bass are not to be taken from Lake Cochituate, in the towns of Natick, Wayland and Framingham, Middlesex County. Trout and pickerel may be taken by line and hook only. Nets or seines with meshes less than five inches prohibited on the Connecticut River and its tributaries. Trespass, Sunday shooting and fishing, the pollution of streams, use of nets, seines, and exportation of game birds or animals, prohibited.

MICHIGAN.—Deer in Upper Peninsula, September 25 to October 25; Lower Peninsula, November 5 to November 25. Killing deer or fawns in red or spotted coat, and in the water, or by means of pitfall or trap or artificial light, forbidden. Hounding prohibited, and dogs found on a

deer track may be killed. Deer and elks protected on Bois Blanc Island
until November 1, 1899. Wild turkeys, November 1 to December 1f.
Woodcocks, August 15 to December 15. (This is the new law, but it does
not take effect until October 1, 1891, therefore the old law is in force
until then, which makes the open season on woodcocks commence September 1. The same is true regarding grouse, which, under the old law,
may be legally killed from September 1 to October 1 and under
the new law as stated herewith.) Lower Peninsula: Ruffed grouse
(partridge), pheasants, quails (Colins or Virginia partridge), November 1
to December 15. Upper Peninsula: Ruffed grouse (partridge). October,
1 to January 1. Snipes and wild geese, red-heads, bluebills, canvas-backs
widgeons and pintail ducks September 1 to May 1. All other wildfowl,
September 1 to January 1. Prairie chickens protected to November, 1894.
No trapping or snaring allowed. No punt or swivel guns allowed. Nests
and eggs of birds protected. Possession, sale or transportation during
close season prohibited. Insectivorous and song birds protected. Exportation of game prohibited. Bounty of three cents per head paid on sparrows. Using guns within five miles of pigeon nestings and netting within
two miles is prohibited. Speckled trout, grayling, California trout, and
landlocked salmon, with hook and line only. May 1 to September 1; less
than six inches in length protected; also protected in streams where they
are not native for three years after first planting; brook trout and graylings shall not be taken for sale or sold. Black, strawberry, green or white
bass at any time, but by hook and line only; mascalonge, July 1 to March,
1. The use of dynamite, herculean or giant powder or other explosives,
seines, pound nets, gill nets, or any species of nets, jacks or artificial
lights of any kind prohibited. There are local laws in several counties
The Governor shall appoint a game and fish warden, to serve four years,
and he in turn shall appoint deputy wardens—not to exceed three in each
county.

MINNESOTA —Deer and elks. November 1 to December 1. Moose,
caribou and reindeer protected until April 20, 1896. Hounding prohibited. Woodcocks, July 4 to November 1. Prairie chickens, sharp-tailed grouse, ruffed grouse or pheasants, quails or partridges, September 1 to November 1. Geese, ducks, brants, snipe and all aquatic fowl,
August 20 to April 25. Minks, muskrats, otters and beavers, November 1
to May 1. All plumage, song and insectivorous birds, their nests and
eggs, and the nests and eggs of game birds protected, excepting blackbirds and sparrows. Trapping, netting, snaring, night hunting and the
use of artificial lights, or other devices, prohibited, except that decoys
may be used to lure ducks, wild geese and brants. Trespass prohibited ;
lands must be posted. Speckled, river or brook trout, April 1 to October
1. Other fish, May 1 to March 1, except where prohibited by local laws.
Hook and line fishing only permitted. Nets, weirs, seines, explosives,
drugs, the pollution of streams, and fish houses on ice, prohibited. Fishing within four hundred feet of any fishway prohibited.

MISSISSIPPI —Deer. September 1 to March 1. Wild turkeys, ruffed grouse and quails, October 1 to May 1. Turtle doves and starlings, September 1 to March 1. Catbirds, mocking-birds and thrushes protected at all times. In Tunica County, the killing or taking of any kind of game bird or animal, fowl or fish for profit, sale or transportation is prohibited until 1897. A land-owner may kill or fish on his own land, or give permission to others, but for immediate use only. Numerous county laws. In Tate County, open season for all kinds of game, November 1 to March 1. Panola County, quails, October 15 to April 15. The law grants the board of supervisors of any county the right to change the State law, at any time. Seines, nets, traps, explosives, drugs, etc., prohibited.

MISSOURI.—Deer, October 1 to January 1; turkeys, September 15 to March 1. Prairie chickens (pinnated grouse), August 15 to February 1. Ruffed grouse (commonly called pheasants) and quails (Virginia partridges), October 1 to January 1. Woodcocks, July 1 to January 10. Waterfowl not protected. Doves, meadow larks and plovers, August 1 to February 1. All insectivorous birds, their nests and eggs, and those of game birds, protected. Possession of game out of season illegal. Birds not showing shot marks to be considered as illegally killed. All railway companies, express companies and carriers are forbidden to carry game out of season. Non-residents forbidden to trap or kill any deer, turkeys, prairie chickens, quails, ruffed grouse, wild geese, brants, wild ducks, snipes, woodcocks, and any furred animal. Shooting on inclosed lands without permission, illegal. Any person may catch or kill on his own premises, for his own or for his own family's consumption, quails or prairie chickens, from October 15 to February 1. Fishing with hook and line at any time. Drugs, poisons, explosives, permanent obstructions, nets, weirs, seines, traps, etc., prohibited, except that a net may be used to catch minnows, and residents may take fish with a seine or set net having meshes not smaller than two inches square from May 1 to April 1.

MONTANA.—Deer, antelopes, mountain sheep, mountain goats, elks and moose, September 15 to January 15. Buffalos and quails protected until 1901. Hunting for skins only, for market or for sale, and hounding prohibited. No close season for bears, curlews and snipes. Otters, martens and fishers, October 1 to April 1. Grouse of all kinds, sage-hens, fool hens, pheasants and partridges, August 15 to November 15. Ducks and geese, August 15 to May 1. Song and insectivorous birds protected; their nests and eggs, and those of all game birds, protected. Hook and line and spear fishing allowed at any time, but catching speckled or mountain trout for profit prohibited; the use of explosives, poisonous drugs and nets, traps, etc., prohibited.

NEBRASKA.—Buffalos, elks, mountain sheep, deer and antelopes, October 1 to January 1. Grouse, September 1 to January 1. Quails and turkeys, October 1 to January 1. Snaring and trapping forbidden. Minks and muskrats, February 15 to April 15. Ducks, geese and woodcocks not protected. Nests and eggs protected. Sneak boats and punt and swivel guns prohibited. Insectivorous and song birds protected. Hounding of deer prohibited in Burt, Washington, Douglas, Sarpy, Cass, Saunders and Dodge counties. Transportation of grouse, quails, turkeys, buffalos, elks, mountain sheep, deer and antelopes prohibited at all times of the year. Fish can be taken with hook and line only. Fish planted by the Fish Commission or private persons protected at all times. Taking fish by any other means than with hook and line prohibited.

NEVADA.—Deer, elks, antelopes, mountain sheep and goats, August 1 to December 1. Partridges, pheasants, woodcocks, geese, woodducks, teals, mallards and other ducks, sandhill cranes, brants, swans, plovers, curlews, snipes, grouse, sharp-tailed grouse, robins, meadow-larks, September 1 to March 15. Sage chickens, August 1 to January 1. Quails, September 1 to January 1. Beavers and otters protected until April, 1897. Insectivorous birds and nests of all birds, protected. Unlawful to construct dams or any river obstruction without proper fishways. Brook trout and landlocked salmon, April 1 to October 1. Lake trout, April 1 to January 1. Fishing with hook and line only permitted. Pollution of streams, use of poisons, drugs, explosives, seines, traps, weirs, etc., prohibited. Trespassing prohibited. No close season for other fish.

NEW HAMPSHIRE.—Deer, moose or caribou, September 1 to January 1. Hunting with dogs prohibited between September 15 and November 1. Not more than one moose, two caribou and three deer permitted to be killed by one person during the open season. Deer protected in Cheshire County until August 14, 1899. Minks, beavers, sables, otters or fishers, October 15 to April 1. Raccoons or gray squirrels, September 1 to January 1. Hares, rabbits or muskrats, September 1 to April 1. Plovers, yellowlegs, sandpipers, ducks or rails, August 1 to February 1. Ruffed grouse, woodcocks and quails, September 1 to January 1. Insectivorous and song birds protected. Nests protected. Snaring or trapping ruffed grouse or quails prohibited. Transportation, possession or sale in close season prohibited. Land-locked or fresh water salmon, April 15 to September 30. Brook and speckled trout, April 15 to September 15. Pike-perch and white perch, July 1 to May 1. Black bass, June 15 to May 1. Mascalonge, pickerel, pike and grayling, June 1 to April 1; pickerel in Lake Warren, May 1 to November 1. Lobsters, September 15 to August 25. Brook trout less than five inches in length protected. In Sunapee Lake, brook, speckled, Loch Levin or rainbow trout of less than ten inches in length, and black bass less than eight inches in length protected. Not more than ten pounds of brook or speckled trout allowed in possession at one time. Striped bass, land-locked salmón, aureolus or golden trout less than ten inches in length protected. Lamper eels, August 1 to May 1, under certain restrictions. Fishing in certain sections of Cockermouth River and Fowler's River prohibited until August 14, 1893. The use of nets, drugs, explosives and sp earing, and the pollution of streams prohibited. The Governor appoints a fish and game commission, not exceeding three in number, and game wardens are appointed for each town. Sunday shooting and trespass prohibited.

NEW JERSEY.—Ruffed grouse, October 1 to December 16. Quails, November 1 to December 16. Woodcocks, October 1 to December 16, and during the month of July. Plovers, August 1 to December 16. Snipes, October 1 to December 16, and during the months of March and April. Prairie chickens, November 1 to January 1. Reed birds, rail birds and marsh hens, August 25 to December 16. Woodducks, September 1 to January 1. Gray and black squirrels, September 15 to December 16. Fox squirrels, September 1 to January 1. Rabbits, November 1 to December 16. Song and insectivorous birds, and nests and eggs of all birds protected. Trapping and snaring prohibited. Salmon trout, March 1 to October 1. Brook trout, April 1 to July 15. Black and Oswego bass, May 30 to December 1. Pickerel and pike, May 1 to March 1. Set lines, nets, seines, or any device obstructing the free passage of fish prohibited. Non-residents must comply with the by-laws of the game protective societies of the State or be debarred from shooting under penalty.

NEW MEXICO.—Elks, buffalos, deer, fawns, antelopes, mountain sheep, wild turkeys, grouse and quails, September 1 to May 1 Not applicable to travelers or persons in camp, whose necessities may compel them to kill for purposes of subsistence. Trout or other food fishes for subsistence only and with hook and line only, June 1 to November 1. The use of poisons, drugs, explosives, nets or similar devices, artificial obstructions and pollution of streams, forbidden.

NEW YORK.—Deer, August 15 to November 1; hounding permitted, from September 1 to October 20, except in Queens and Suffolk counties where it is lawful only the first ten days of October, exclusive of Sundays; in St. Lawrence and Delaware counties hounding is prohibited at all times; moose and fawns protected. But three deer can be taken in one season, and one only may be transported when accompanied by the owner. Crusting and yarding of deer prohibited. Ducks, geese and brants, September 1 to May 1; in the waters of Long Island, October 1 to May 1; in Chautauqua County, September 1 to February 1. Night hunting and use of artificial light, punt or swivel gun and nets prohibited. Use of floating batteries, etc., prohibited; and bough houses and decoys must be within twenty rods from the shore, except in Great South Bay west of Smith's Point, Peconic Bay, Shennecock Bay, Lake Ontario,

River St. Lawrence and the Hudson River below Albany. Shooting from sail or steam boats prohibited, except on Long Island Sound, Gardner's and Peconic Bays, Lake Ontario and Hudson River below Iona Island. Quails, November 1 to January 1. On Robins Island, October 15 to February 1. Rabbits and hares, November 1 to February 1. Hunting with ferrets prohibited. Woodcocks, ruffed grouse and prairie chickens, September 1 to January 1. Snipes, sandpipers and plovers, July 10 to January 1 in counties of Queens and Suffolk. Rail birds and meadow hens, in counties of Queens and Suffolk, September 1 to January 1. Netting and snaring prohibited. Squirrels, August 1 to February 1; in Cortland County, September 1 to January 1. Song and insectivorous birds protected. Nests protected. Robins and blackbirds may be shot on Long Island and Staten Island from November 1 to January 1. English sparrows, crows, blackbirds, hawks and owls not protected. Speckled, brook, California and brown trout, April 1 to September 1; in Forest Preserve, May 1 to September 15; Steuben County, May 1 to August 1. If less than six inches in length must be returned to waters where caught. Lake trout, salmon trout and land-locked salmon same as speckled trout, except in Forest Preserve, May 1 to October 1; and in inland waters, April 1 to October 1; Lake George, May 1 to October 1. Salmon, March 1 to August 15, with hook and line, angling by hand only. Black bass, May 30 to January 1, except in Oneida Lake, June 1 to March 1; and Lake Mahopac, Schroon Lake and River, Paradox Lake, Friends' Lake, Skaneateles Lake, Lake Erie and Niagara River above the falls, July 1 to January 1; Lake George and Brant Lake, August 1 to January 1; St. Lawrence, Clyde, Seneca and Oswego rivers, lakes Ontario, Conesus and Black, May 20 to January 1; Lake Champlain, June 15 to January 1; Glen Lake, July 10 to January 1. All black bass weighing less than one-half pound or less than eight inches in length protected; this restriction applies also to Oswego bass caught in Glen Lake and fresh water striped bass. Mascalonge and pike-perch, May 30 to January 1; St. Lawrence, Clyde, Seneca and Oswego rivers, lakes Ontario, Conesus and Black, May 20 to January 1; Oneida Lake, May 30 to March 1; Lake Champlain, June 15 to January 1; Erie County, July 1 to January 1. Oswego bass, same as mascalonge, except in Glen Lake, July 10 to January 1. Fresh water striped bass, May 20 to January 1; Erie County, July 1 to January 1. Salt water striped bass, no close season; protected in Jamaica Bay under six inches in length; in other waters size same as black bass. Sea bass and tautogs under six inches in length protected in Jamaica Bay. Pike, Lake Champlain, June 15 to January 1. Pickerel, Lake George and Glen Lake, July 1 to February 15; Lake Champlain, June 15 to January 1. Shad, Hudson River, March 15 to June 15; none allowed to be taken above the northern line of Westchester County from sunset on Saturday to sunrise on the following Monday. Bullheads, Lake George and Glen Lake, July 1 to April 1. The Forest Preserve includes portions of the counties of Clinton, Delaware, Essex, Franklin, Fulton, Hamiton, Herkimer, Lewis, Oneida, St. Lawrence, Saratoga, Warren, Washington, Greene, Ulster and Sullivan. The State is divided into fifteen game and fish protection districts. Protectors appointed for each district.

NORTH CAROLINA.—A new law has been passed, regulating the open season in the several counties of the State. We have not received a copy of it up to the time of going to press, but will publish a synopsis of it in a subsequent issue.

NORTH DAKOTA.—Buffalos, elks, deer, antelopes and mountain sheep, September 1 to January 1. Grouse of all kinds, September 1 to January 1. Ducks, snipes, geese, brants, plovers and curlews, September 1 to May 1. Not more than twenty-five of any of the game birds or fowl mentioned allowed to be killed or had in possession at any one time. Their nests and eggs protected. Exportation of game prohibited; not more than one dozen of either of said birds allowed to be shipped or transported in any one day within the State by any one person, after making affidavit that said birds have been legally killed. Shoulder guns only allowed; all other devices, poisons, traps, etc., prohibited. Wasting game or leaving the same lying about, prohibited. Pike, pickerel, perch, bass, mascalonge, May 1 to February 1. Fishing with hook and line only allowed; all other devices prohibited.

OHIO.—Deer, October 15 to November 20. Quails, November 10 to December 15. Squirrels, July 1 to December 15. Woodcocks, July 15 to November 1. Buffed grouse or pheasants and prairie chickens, September 1 to December 15. Ducks, September 1 to April 10. Turkeys, October 1 to December 15. Trapping or snaring quails or partridges prohibited. The use of any other gun than a shoulder gun, artificial light, sink boat or battery, steam or naphtha launch, net or trap, prohibited. Nests and eggs of all game birds and fowl protected. Ducks shall not be hunted on Sunday, Monday and Tuesday of any week between September 1 and April 10. Sunday hunting prohibited at all times. Swans, insectivorous birds and their nests protected at all times. Disturbing pigeon roosts or discharging any firearm at any wild pigeon within one-half mile of a wild pigeon roost, prohibited. The use of ferrets for catching rabbits on the premises of another, prohibited. Muskrats, minks, and otters, March 1 to April 15. Brook trout, salmon, land-locked salmon, or California salmon, March 14 to September 15. With these exceptions there are no restrictions to fishing with hook and line, with bait or lure, except that bass under eight inches in length, and fish in private or posted waters are protected. Netting and seining are allowed in many waters subject to specific or local laws. Explosives, poisonous drugs, spearing, shooting, trespassing, and selling or having in possession any kind of fish in close season, prohibited. Spearing suckers is allowed in all streams flowing into Lake Erie.

OREGON.—Male deer or buck, July 1 to November 1; female deer or doe, August 1 to January 1; spotted fawns protected; neither male nor female deer can be killed at any time for other than food purposes. Elks, moose and mountain sheep, August 1 to November 1; shall not be killed for other than food purposes; wilds swans and ducks, September 1 to March 1; ducks can be killed at any time to protect growing crops; grouse, pheasants, mongolian pheasants, quails or partridges, September 1 to November 15; netting and snaring quails, prairie chickens and ruffed grouse, or having the same in possession alive, prohibited; nests and eggs of game birds and wildfowl protected. Ring-neck Mongolian pheasants, Tragopan pheasants, silver pheasants and golden pheasants protected. Mountain or brook trout, April 1 to November 1. Red-fish and lake trout, January 1 to August 10. Salmon protected in the Columbia River during March, August, September and during the weekly close times in April, May, June and July, i..e., from 6 p. m. Saturday to 6 p. m. Sunday; taking them with any other device than hook and line prohibited in any other waters, April 1 to November 15. Fishing near fishways, drugs, explosives, nets, pollution of streams, etc., and trespass, prohibited.

PENNSYLVANIA.—Elks and deer October 1 to December 15; but owing to an error, it is illegal to have deer in possession after November 30 The killing of fawns when in spotted coat, chasing of elks or deer with hounds, and the killing of deer when in the water prohibited. Squirrels, September 1 to January 1. Hares or rabbits, November 1 to January 1. Hunting or killing of rabbits with ferrets prohibited. Wild turkeys, October 15 to January 1. Plovers, July 15 to January 1. Woodcocks, July 4 to January 1. Quails, November 1 to December 15. Ruffed and pinnated grouse, October 1 to January 1. Rails or reed birds, September 1 to December 1. Wildfowl, September 1 to May 1. Insectivorous birds protected, except English sparrows. Pigeon nestings protected against firearms to a radius of one-fourth mile from roosting or breeding place, and penalty for disturbance in any manner while nesting; and snaring or netting for the purpose of killing during the nesting season prohibited. Snaring, netting or catching of game birds by torchlight prohibited. Sunday hunting and shooting prohibited Shooting of wildfowl limited to use of shoulder gun only. Sea salmon, April 1 to July 1 Speckled trout. April 15 to July 15; under five inches in length protected. Lake trout, January 1 to October 1. Black, green, yellow, willow, rock, Lake Erie and grass bass, pike, pickerel, and wall-eyed pike or Susquehanna salmon, June 1 to January 1. Bass less than six inches in length protected. German carp, September 1 to May 1. Artificially stocked streams protected for three years after stocking. Hook and line fishing only allowed; use of nets or traps of any kind, poisons etc., prohibited.

RHODE ISLAND.—Woodcocks, ruffed grouse or partridges, September 1 to January 1. Quails, October 1 to January 1. Bartram's tattlers or grass plovers, August 1 to April 1. Dusky or black ducks, wood or Summer ducks, and blue or green-winged teals, September 1 to March 1, grouse or heath-hen, November 1 to January 1. Trapping prohibited, and shoulder guns only allowed. Squirrels, rabbits and hares, September 1 to January 1; use of ferrets or weasels to catch rabbits or hares forbidden. Wild pigeons, August 10 to January 1. Eggs and nests protected. All fresh water ducks other than those before mentioned, all sea ducks, geese, crows, kingfishers, crow blackbirds, herons, bitterns, plovers (except as mentioned above), curlews, rails, sandpipers, snipes and all birds of prey except fish-hawks, or ospreys, may be killed at any time. Trout, March 1 to August 15; less than six inches in length protected at all times. Black bass protected until 1893; after that, July 15 to March 1. Hook and line fishing only allowed

SOUTH CAROLINA.—Deer, September 1 to February 1, except in the counties of Clarendon Georgetown, Colleton, Williamsburg, Marlboro, Kershaw, Harry, Darlington, Marion and Berkeley, where it is August 1 to February 1. Wild turkeys, ruffed grouse, woodcocks and quails or partridges, November 1 to April 1. Doves, August 1 to March 1. Insectivorous birds protected. Fire-hunting prohibited. Non-residents

SOUTH DAKOTA.—Prairie chickens, ruffed and sharp-tailed grouse, August 15 to January 1. Snipes, plovers, curlews and waterfowl, Sep. tember 1 to May 15. Quails protected until February 3, 1893. Song and insectivorous birds protected. Netting and trapping prohibited. Shooting of more than twenty-five birds of one kind in a day or the possession of the same prohibited. Shipping out of State, and the shipment of more than twelve birds within the State, prohibited. Deer, buffalos, elks, antelopes and mountain sheep, September 1 to January 1. In the counties of Clay, Union and Lincoln, deer from October 1 to January 1. Bass, mascalonge, pike, pickerel and perch, May 1 to February 1. Those intended for breeding may be taken at any time. Netting prohibited except in the Missouri and Red rivers. Shipment out of the State of carcass of buffalo, elk, deer, antelope or mountain sheep prohibited.

TENNESSEE.—In counties of Anderson, Cheatham, Coffee, Davidson, Dickson, Fayette, Fentress, Giles, Grundy, Hamblen, Hamilton, Hancock, Hardeman, Haywood, Henry, Houston, Jefferson, Knox, Lake, Lincoln, London, McMinn, Madison, Monroe, Montgomery, Obion, Roane, Rutherford, Sevier, Shelby, Stewart, Sullivan, Sumner, Tipton, Trousdale, Unicol, Williamson and Wilson, unlawful to kill or hunt deer for profit, except that citizens may kill deer for profit on their own lands from August 1 to January 1, and during that period may hunt or kill deer for their own consumption. Unlawful in these counties for any person to hunt, net, trap or capture any quail or partridge except from November 1 to March 1, and not then for profit, except that, during that season, a citizen may do so for profit on his own land but not elsewhere. Netting quails at any season by any person prohibited in said counties. In counties of Scott; Fentress, Pickett, Morgan, Cumberland, Bledsoe, Sequatchie, Van Buren, White, Putnam, Rhea, Clay, Campbell, Henry. Johnson, Carter, Sullivan, Meigs, Claiborne, Grundy, James, Overton, Marion, Roane, and Warren unlawful for non-residents to hunt, kill, catch or capture any species of game or fish, and unlawful for any person to hunt or kill any species of game for profit. Morgan County, deer and wild turkeys, October 1 to December 1. Benton and Humphreys counties, deer, September 1 to January 1. Dyer, Maury, and Bedford counties, deer, September 1 to March 1. Pheasants, grouse, quails, partridges, larks, woodcocks, and snipes, September 15 to March 1; wild turkeys, September 15 to May 1; song and insectivorous birds and nests protected. Unlawful to trap or net game. Robertson and Maury counties, wild turkeys, partridges, quails, grouse, pheasants, woodcocks, snipes and larks, September 1 to February 1. Shelby County, squirrels, September 1 to February 1; nests and eggs protected. Montgomery and Cheatham counties, grouse or pheasants and larks, October 15 to March 1; woodcocks, doves and wild turkeys, August 1 to March 1; snipes, plovers or ducks, September 1 to May 1. Johnson, Carter, Washington, Greene and Marion counties, partridges, quails, woodcocks, pheasants and wild turkeys, October 1 to April 1; Unicoi, Hamilton, Henry and Haywood counties, woodcocks, pheasants and wild turkeys, October 1 to April 1; unlawful to export game mentioned from these counties beyond the limits of the State; this does not apply to persons killing game on their own premises. Johnson and Carter counties, deer protected. Bedford County, partridges may be trapped or netted September 15 to March 1; wild turkeys may be trapped September 15 to May 1. The use of dynamite, giant powder, explosive or any other substance, other than angling with hook and line prohibited. Use of hand or minnow net for taking small fish or minnows for bait allowed.

TEXAS.—Deer, June 1 to December 1. Wild turkeys, September 1 to May 15. Prairie chickens, August 1 to March 1. Quails and partridges, October 1 to April 1. Song and insectivorous birds protected. No seining, trapping or netting of fish permitted above tidewater from February 1 to July 1. Use of nets or seins with meshes less than two and one-half inches square, drugs, explosives and poisons, prohibited. Owing to their being too thinly settled or unorganized, these provisions do not apply to the counties of Anderson, Andrews, Angelina, Archer, Armstrong Atascosa, Bailey, Baylor, Bell, Borden, Bosque, Brazos, Briscoe, Brown, Callahan, Cameron, Camp, Carson, Cass, Castro, Cherokee, Childres, Clay, Cochran, Collin, Collingsworth, Comanche, Cooke, Coryell, Cottle, Crosby,

Dallam, Dawson, Deaf Smith, Delta, Dickens, Dimmitt, Donley, Easland, Ellis, Erath, Fisher, Floyd, Franklin, Freestone, Frio, Gaines, Garza, Gonzales, Gray, Greer, Gaudulupe, Grimes, Hale, Hall, Hamilton, Hansford, Hardeman, Hartley, Haskell, Hemphill, Hockley, Hood, Hopkins, Howard, Hunt, Hutchinson, Jack, Jackson, Jones, Karnes, Kent, King, Kinney, Knox, Lamb, Lipscomb, Lubbock, Lynn, Martin, Maverick, Mitchell, Montague, Montgomery, Moore, Morris, Motley, Nacogdoches, Nolan, Ochiltree, Oldham, Palo Pinto, Parmer, Polk, Potter, Rains, Randall, Robert, Robertson Rockwall. Runnells, Sabine, San Augustine, San Jacinto, Scurry, Shackleford, Shelby, Sherman, Smith, Somervell, Stephens, Stonewall, Swisher, Taylor, Terry, Throckmorton, Titus, Upshur, Van Zandt, Walker, Wheeler, Wichita, Wilbarger, Wilson, Wise, Wood, Young, Yoakum, Zavalla. Houston protects Quails, only, as above. Fannin County protects prairie chickens, quails and insectivorous birds, as above. Lee and Fayette protect turkeys, prairie chickens and quails, as above. Bastrop and Brazoria protect deer, turkeys, prairie chickens and quails, is above. Kaufman protects quails and insectivorous birds, as above. Bowie protects deer and turkeys, as above.

UTAH.—Elks, deer, buffalos or bisons, antelopes and mountain sheep, September 1 to December 1. Hounding prohibited; dogs in pursuit of above animals may be legally killed. Hide and skin hunting, the exportation of game animals or fish, or having in possession during the close season, prohibited. Quails, partridges, pheasants, prairie chickens and sage-hens or grouse, August 15 to March 15. Wild geese, ducks and snipes, September 1 to April 1. Night hunting and trapping prohibited. Insectivorous birds, the English sparrow and blackbird excepted, protected. Nests protected. Trout, June 15 to February 15. Trout less than six inches in length protected. Imported fish protected. Seining, with lawful size meshes, in Bear and Utah Lakes, October 1 to March 1; in Green River at any time. The use of set lines, nets, seines, weirs, dams or other artificial obstructions, poisons, drugs and explosives of any kind, prohibited. Indians are not exempt from the laws except on their reservations.

VERMONT.—Gray squirrels, September 1 to February 1. Quails and ruffed grouse, September 1 to February 1. Hunting ruffed grouse with dogs prohibited. Woodcocks, August 15 to February 1. Wildfowl, September 1 to February 1, except woodducks. Nests and eggs, protected, and trapping and snaring forbidden. Insectivorous birds, eggs and nests protected. Sunday shooting prohibited. Deer protected until 1900. Minks, beavers, fishers and otters, November 1 to April 1. Trout, land-locked salmon, salmon trout or longe, May 1 to September 1. Trout, land-locked salmon and salmon trout less than six inches in length, protected. Black bass, June 1 to February 1. Black bass less than ten inches in length, protected. Whitefish or lake shad, November 15 to

November 1. Wall-eyed pike, pike-perch, June 1 to February 1. Fishing allowed with hook and line only All other devices prohibited. Local laws govern many waters

VIRGINIA —The game and fish laws of Virginia are so complicated that it is almost impossible to compile an intelligible synopsis of them, the State law not being in force in the majority of counties owing to local enactments. A license in writing must be obtained from the owner or tenant of any land or watercourse. Non-residents prohibited from killing any wildfowl below the head of tidewater. Night shooting and shooting from skiffs, floats or sink boxes prohibited Deer, August 15 to January 1; Essex County, August 15 to February 1; Frederick and Shenandoah counties, September 15 to December 15; King and Queen counties, August 15 to February 1; King William County October 1 to February 1; Lancaster and Richmond counties, October 15 to February 1. Protected in Page County; Rockingham County, October 1 to November 15 Hounding prohibited by State and county laws, with slight exceptions. Pheasants or ruffed grouse and turkeys, Sepember 15 to February 1, in the counties west of the Blue Ridge (except Rockbridge), and in Rockbridge and counties east of the Blue Ridge (except Prince Edward), October 15 to January 15; Prince Edward County, October 15 to March 1. Turkeys, Frederick and Shenandoah counties, November 1 to February 1; Isle of Wight, Nansemond and Southampton counties, September 15 to February 15; King and Queen counties, August 15 to February 1; King William County, November 1 to March 15. Wild fowl (except Summer ducks), September 15 to May 1. Woodcocks, November 1 to April 1; Frederick and Shenandoah counties, July 1 to April 1; Alexandria and Fairfax counties, July 4 to January 1; Loudon County, June 15 to January 1. Partridges or quails in the following counties as noted herewith: From October 15 to January 15: Albemarle, Alexandria, Buckingham, Buchanan, Campbell, Charles City, Charlotte, Chesterfield, Culpeper, Elizabeth City, Fairfax, Fauquier, Fluvanna, Gloucester, Goochland Greene, James City, King George, King William, Louisa, Madison, Matthews, Middlesex, Nelson, New Kent, Northumberland, Orange, Patrick, Pittsylvania, Powhatan, Prince George, Prince William, Rappahannock, Spotsylvania, Stafford, Surry, Warwick, Westmoreland, York. From October 15 to January 1: Bland, Botetourt, Carroll, Craig, Dickinson, Floyd, Giles, Lee, Loudon, Montgomery, Page, Pulaski, Roanoke, Russell, Rockingham, Tazewell, Wise, Warren. From October 15 to March 1: Prince Edward. From October 15 to February 1: Lancaster, Richmond. From October 15 to February 15: Halifax, Hanover Henrico, King and Queen. From October 31 to December 25: Clarke. From November 1 to January 1: Frederick, Shenandoah. From November 1 to February 15: Henry, Nansemond, Isle of Wight, Southampton. From November 1 to March 1: King William. From November 1 to

February 1: Accomac, Alleghany, Amherst, Augusta, Bath, Bedford, Caroline, Essex, Franklin, Grayson, Highland, Northampton, Norfolk, Rockbridge, Scott, Smyth, Washington, Wythe. From November 15 to February 15: Princess Anne. The counties of Amelia, Appomattox, Brunswick, Cumberland, Dinwiddie, Greensville. Lunenburg, Mecklenburg, Nottoway and Sussex, have no law on the subject. Mountain trout, April 1 to September 15. Bass of any kind, July 1 to May 15. Hook and line fishing only allowed. Nets, traps, weirs, obstructions to free passage of fish, drugs, poisons, pollution of streams, etc., prohibited. Local laws regulate fishing in the proximity of dams, junctions, mill ponds, etc.

WASHINGTON.—Deer, moose, elks, mountain sheep and mountain goats, for food purposes only, August 15 to January 1. Hide and head hunting prohibited. Hounding elks or moose except during October, November and December, prohibited. Hounding deer prohibited at all times. Swans and wild ducks of any kind, August 15 to April 1. Prairie chickens, mountain grouse, blue grouse, pintail grouse, pheasants and sagehens, August 1 to January 1. California and Bob White quails, October 1 to January 15. Trapping and snaring prohibited. Nests and eggs of all game birds and fowl protected at all times. Night hunting prohibited. Shooting with swivel or pivot guns, or from sink boxes, rafts, sneak boats, or other devices, except from shore blinds or over decoys, prohibited. Brook trout, mountain trout, bull trout and salmon trout, May 1 to November 1; with hook and line only. Fishing for salmon within one mile below any obstruction erected to obtain fish for propagation, or use of nets, weirs, seines, traps or other similar devices, drugs, explosives, etc., prohibited. Trespass prohibited; lands and waters must be posted. Fish planted in waters protected for three years after planting. Salmon, in Columbia River and tributaries, April 10 to August 10 and September 10 to March 1; protected at all times between 6 p. m. Saturday and 6 p. m. following Sunday. Gray's Harbor, Shoalwater Bay and tributaries, December 15 to November 15. Puget Sound, June 1 to March 1. Pollution of streams prohibited, and dams must have fishways. From and after January 1, 1892, foreigners and non-residents prohibited from taking for sale or profit any salmon, sturgeon or other food fish. Fish commissioner appointed, with salary of $2,000 and expenses. Game warden and deputies appointed by the Governor.

WEST VIRGINIA.—Quails, November 1 to December 20. Wild turkeys, September 15 to January 1. Ruffed and pinnated grouse, November 1 to January 1. Snipes, March 1 to July 1. Woodcocks, July 1 to September 15. Wild ducks, geese and brants, October 1 to April 1. Deer, September 15 to December 15. Insectivorous and song birds, their nests, and eggs, and those of game birds and waterfowl, protected. Snaring, netting or trapping, and the use of swivel or pivot guns, or sneak or push boats, forbidden. Hounding deer prohibited until June, 1892. Trout and land-locked salmon, January 1 to September 1. Jack salmon or white salmon, June 15 to April 1. Nets, weirs, traps, obstructions, poisons, drugs, explosives and trespass, prohibited.

WISCONSIN.—Woodcocks, quails (except in Walworth, Rock, Jefferson, Waukesha, Milwaukee, and Racine counties, where quails, their nests and eggs are protected until September 1, 1894), partridges, pheasants or ruffed grouse, prairie chickens, sharp-tailed grouse, or grouse of any other variety, snipe, plovers, mallard, teal or wood ducks, September 1 to December 1. Wild ducks of any other variety, wild geese or brants of any variety, or any aquatic fowls whatever, September 1 to May 1. Hunting quails or any kind of grouse (partridge, pheasant, or prairie chicken) with dogs prohibited until September 1, 1893. Squirrels, August 1 to December 1. Deer, November 1 to December 1. Hounding or worrying deer prohibited at all times. Snaring, netting, trapping, spring guns, pivot guns, swivel guns, or any similar contrivance, or any firearm other than a shoulder gun, prohibited. Sneak boats, scull boats, sailboats, steamboats or floating rafts or boxes, or any similar device; or any blinds in open water outside the natural growth of grass or rushes, prohibited. Otters, martens, and fishes, November 1 to May 1. The use of dogs or ferrets, nets, traps, snares, clubs or sticks, in the taking or killing of hares or rabbits, prohibited. Eggs and nests of wild pigeons, game and song and insectivorous birds protected. Pigeons protected within three miles of their roost. English sparrows not protected. Brook, rainbow and mountain trout, April 15 to September 1. Mackinaw (lake) trout, January 15 to October 1. Pike (wall-eyed), May 1 to March 1. Black, green and Oswego bass, and mascalonge, May 1 to February 1. Hook and line only. Whitefish may be taken in inland waters with a dip-net having a hoop not exceeding thirty inches in diameter from November 10 to December 15. With this exception the use of any gill, fyke, pound, seine, dip or other net or snare is prohibited in the inland lakes, rivers or streams of the State. Minnows, shiners, chubs, dace, suckers or stickle-backs may be caught for bait in quantities not exceeding one-half bushel in measure, at any one time, by means of a dip-net or seine, except in streams or waters inhabited by or containing trout of any variety. No such fish caught for bait allowed to be shipped out of the State. The use of dynamite or other explosives, and the pollution waters with sawdust, fish offal, etc., prohibited. Spearing prohibited, except in the waters of the Mississippi River and sloughs, Lake Winnebago, Fox and Wolf rivers, and all waters emptying into Green Bay, where sturgeons and pickerel only may be speared. Catching brook, rainbow or mountain trout for sale, out of public waters, is prohibited. The sale of any wall-eyed pike, black bass and frog bass, of less than one pound each, prohibited. It is unlawful for any person to have in his possession to exceed ten pounds of wall-eyed pike, black bass or frog bass weighing less than one pound each. Entering on posted preserves without consent of owner is trespass. Local laws are in force in many counties. A paid State game and fish warden, to hold office for two years, is appointed by the Governor. He may appoint as many deputies as he desires, the latter to receive constable's fees for performance of duty.

WYOMING.—Partridges, pheasants, prairie chickens, prairie hens or grouse, August 15 to November 1. Sage chickens, July 15 to September 15. Snipes, green shanks, tatlers, godwits, curlews, avocets, or other waders, plovers, quails, larks, whip-poor-wills, finches, thrushes, snow_ birds, turkeys, buzzards, robins or other insectivorous birds, protected at all times. Wild ducks, August 1 to May 1. Deer, elks, moose, mountain sheep, mountain goats, antelopes, protected at all times, except that a *bona fide* resident may at any time kill not more than three of any of said animals in any one week, for the purpose only of supplying himself and family with food. Non-residents prohibited from hunting them at any time. Bison or buffalos and beavers protected until March 15, 1900· Exportation of game, hides or heads prohibited. Any game brought into the State must be accompanied by an affidavit, to be recorded in the office of the county clerk and recorder of the county, to prove that said game was not killed in any other State or Territory in violation of the laws of such State or Territory. Trapping and netting prohibited. · Justices of the peace are empowered to appoint special game constables.

BRITISH POSSESSIONS.

QUEBEC.—Moose and caribou, September 1 to February 1. Deer, October 1 to January 1. Hounding, snaring and trapping prohibited. Unless a special permit is first obtained from the Commissioner of Crown Lands, no person (Indian not exempted) shall kill more than two moose three caribous and four deer during the hunting season. After the first ten days of the close season transportation of any game prohibited. Beavers, minks, otters, martens and pekans, November 1 to April 1, Muskrats, in counties of Maskinonge, Yamaska, Richelieu and Berthier, April 1 to M 'y 1. Hares, November 1 to February 1. Woodcocks, snipes and partridges, September 1 to February 1. Ducks of all kinds, September 1 to May 1. Other birds, except eagles, falcons, hawks, wild pigeons, kingfishers, crows, ravens, waxwings, shrikes, jays, magpies, sparrows and starlings, September 1 to March 1. Guns of larger than 8-bore prohibited. Snaring and trapping, except of partridges, prohibited. Night hunting and exportation of game prohibited. Nests and eggs protected. A license required for persons not residents of Quebec or Ontario to hunt or fish. Salmon, February 1 to August 15. Ouananiche, December 1 to September 15 Speckled trout, January 1 to October 1. Gray trout and lunge, December 1 to October 15. Pickerel, May 15 to April 15. Bass and mascalonge, June 15 to April 15. Whitefish, December 1 to November 10. Fishing with hook and line only permitted.

ONTARIO.—Deer, October 15 to November 20. Moose, elks, reindeer or caribous entirely protected until October 15, 1895. Prior to 1895 no person not a resident of Ontario or Quebec for three months shall at any time kill or hunt deer, elks, moose, reindeer or caribous; neither shall any person kill more than five deer in one year, hunting parties of two not more than eight, and hunting parties of three or more not more than twelve. Grouse, pheasants, prairie fowls and partridges, September 1 to January 1. Quails and turkeys, October 15 to December 15. Woodcocks, August 15 to January 1. Snipes, rails and plovers, September 1 to January 1. Ducks, September 1 to January 1. Swans and geese, September 1 to May 1. Hares, September 1 to March 15. Quails cannot be sold, bought or bartered for in any way. Beavers, minks, muskrats, martens, raccoons, otters or fishers, November 1 to May 1. Trapping, snaring, swivel guns, poisoned baits, etc., night shooting, and trespass, prohibited. Insectivorous birds, their nests and eggs, and those of all game birds, protected. Salmon, trout and whitefish, December 1 to November 1. Fresh water herring. December 1 to October 15. Speckled, river and brook trout, May 1 to September 15. Bass and mascalonge.

June 15 to April 15. Pickerel (dore), May 15 to April 15. Use of nets, explosives, spears or grapple hooks prohibited.

MANITOBA.—All kinds of deer, including cabri or antelopes, elks or wapiti, moose, reindeer and caribous, or their fawns, October 1 to December 1. Grouse, partridges, prairie chickens and pheasants, September 1 to December 1. Woodcocks, plovers (except golden plovers), snipes and sandpipers, August 1 to January 1. Any kind of wild duck, sea duck, widgeon, teal, wild swan, or wild goose, except the variety of wild goose commonly known as "the wavey" or "snow goose," September 1 to May 1. Nests and eggs of game birds protected. Otters, fishers, pekans, beavers, muskrats and sables, October 1 to May 15. Martens, November 1 to April 15. Trapping and netting, excepting of otters, fishers, beavers muskrats, martens and pekans, prohibited. Poisons, batteries, swivel guns, sunken punts and night lights and spring guns prohibited. Exportation of game birds and animals, without a permit, prohibited. Hunting on lands without permission of owner forbidden. Insectivorous birds, nests and egg protected. Sunday shooting prohibited. Transportation of game forbidden during the close season. Non-residents prohibited from shooting unless provided with a license (costing $25). Pickerel (doré), May 15 to April 16. Speckled trout, January 1 to October 1. Explosives and poisons prohibited.

BRITISH COLUMBIA.—Deer, elks, reindeer, caribou, mountain goats, mountain sheep and hares, August 15 to December 20. Cow elks protected at all times. Grouse, partridges, prairie fowl, California and Virginia quails, robins and meadow larks, September 1 to February 1. Wild ducks, September 1 to March 1. Cock pheasants, October 1 to February 1. Hen pheasants protected at all times. Night hunting prohibited. Hounding deer prohibited except east of the Cascades. Cock pheasants and quails are protected on the mainland until September 1, 1894 ; may be shot as above stated on Vancouver Island. Insectivorous birds and their nests protected. Gulls protected in the harbors and tributary streams of Victoria, Esquimault, New Westminster, Nanaimo or Vancouver. Skin hunting and exporting prohibited. The sale of any pheasant, fawn or deer under the age of twelve months, and does of any age, prohibited. A non-resident must procure a license to shoot game animals. Trout, March 15 to October 16. Nets, weirs, seines, or similar devices, explosives, drugs and poisons prohibited

NEW BRUNSWICK.—Moose (bull), deer and caribou, September 1 to January 15. Cow moose are protected absolutely. Partridges or ruffed grouse, September 20 to December 1. Snipes, September 15 to March 1. Woodcocks and teal ducks, September 1 to December 1. Geese, ducks and brants, September 1 to May 1. Hares and rabbits, September 1 to March 1. Mink, otter, fisher, sable and beaver, September 1 to May 1. Night hunting by artificial light and use of swivel or punt gun prohibited. Non-residents prohibited to hunt without a license. Hounding moose, caribou and deer prohibited. Sunday shooting and exportation of game prohibited. No person or party is allowed to kill more than one moose, two caribous or three red deer during any one season. Sea-gulls protected in the parish of Grand Manan. Bass, October 1 to March 1. Bass of less than two pounds, protected. Salmon, March 1 to August 15. Fly fishing for salmon, August 15 to February 1. Speckled trout and land-locked salmon, May 1 to September 15. Explosives, nets, traps, etc., prohibited.

NOVA SCOTIA.—Moose and caribou, September 15 to February 1. Hares or rabbits, October 1 to March 1. Otter and mink, November 1 to May 1. Beavers, and furred animals, November 1 to April 1. Grouse or partridge, September 15 to January 1. Woodcocks, snipes and teal ducks, August 20 to March 1. Blue-wing and black ducks, August 1 to April 1. Woodcocks must not be shot before sunrise or after sunset. No person shall kill more than two moose or four caribou in one season. Pheasants protected. Song and insectivorous birds protected. Non-residents prohibited to hunt without a license. Exportation of game or hides prohibited. Bass fishing at any time with hook and line only ; bass under two pounds weight protected. Salmon, March 1 to August 15 ; fly fishing, February 1 to August 15. Speckled trout, lake trout or land-locked salmon, April 1 to October 1. Explosives, traps, nets, etc., prohibited.

NEWFOUNDLAND Moose and elks protected until January 1, 1896. Caribou, October 1 to February 15. Not more than five stag and three hind caribou allowed to be killed in any one season. Deer, July 15 to March 1. Rabbits or hares, September 1 to March 1 Otters and beavers, October 1 to April 1. Curlews, plovers, snipes, or other wild or migratory birds (excepting wild geese), August 20 to January 12. Grouse or partridge, September 15 to January 12. Wild geese, August 29 to April 1. Capercailzie protected. License for non-resident required. Sunday shooting and exportation of game prohibited. Trout char, whitefish, land locked salmon, or any fresh water or any migratory fish, December 1 to September 15. Salmon, May 1 to September 10. Nets, traps, weirs, explosives, etc., prohibited. License required.

NORTHWEST TERRITORIES. Elks, moose, caribou, antelopes, deer, mountain sheep or goat, hares, September 1 to February 1. Snipes, August 15 to May 1. Grouse, partridges, pheasants, prairie chickens, September 1 to February 1. Ducks and geese, August 15 to May 15. Snaring, trapping, baiting, etc., prohibited. Exportation prohibited Game may be killed at any time to prevent starvation, but not more than immediate want demands. Pickerel, May 15 to April 15 Speckled trout, January 1 to October 1. Explosives, nets, etc., prohibited.

PRINCE EDWARD'S ISLAND —Partridges or ruffed grouse, October 1 to February 15. Woodcocks and snipes, August 20 to January 1. Ducks, August 10 to March 1. Night shooting, sneak boats, or any similar devices, prohibited. Trout, December 1 to October 1, with hook and line only.

AMERICAN RULES

FOR TRAP SHOOTING.

Adopted by the National Gun Association.

RULE 6. *Use of Second Barrel.*—Where special matches are arranged, allowing the use of both barrels at single birds, a kill or break with the second barrel shall be scored one-half.

RULE 7. *Scoring Incorrect Handicap.*—No member is to shoot at a distance nearer than that at which he is handicapped. If he does so, the first time the shot shall be scored "no bird;" the second time it shall be scored a "lost bird;" and the third time he shall forfeit all rights in the contest, and be barred from all other contests during the same meeting, and be subject to such additional fines and penalties as the Constitution and By-Laws may provide.

RULE 8. *Closing of Entries.*—All entries shall close at the firing of the first gun. In large international or interstate tournaments, all entries for the first match each day shall be made before 6 P. M. of the day preceding the shoot, by depositing 10 per cent of the entrance fee, which shall be forfeited to the management if the entry is not completed before the firing of the first gun. •

RULE 9. *Class Shooting.*—All sweepstakes shall be Class Shooting unless otherwise specified.

RULE 10. *Names Claimed.*—The Secretary shall keep a book in which he shall record the names of all the members who desire to shoot under an assumed name, and record the name assumed by each. He shall make a charge of 50 cents, and no more, for each name recorded. No two members shall shoot under the same assumed name. The Secretary may, at the request of a member, issue the handicap card to him, bearing his assumed title only.

RULE 11. *Score with Ink only.*—All scoring shall be done with ink or indelible pencil. The scoring of a "lost bird" shall be indicated by a "0;" of a "dead" or "broken" bird by a "1."

ART. III.—THE TRAPS.

RULE 12. *Arrangement of Traps.*—Five traps shall be used. They shall be set level upon the ground, without any inequalities of setting in either, in an arc of a circle, five yards apart. The radius of the circle shall be eighteen yards. The traps shall be numbered from No. 1, upon the left, to No. 5, upon the right, consecutively. In all traps, except No. 3, the fourth notch, or a maximum velocity equivalent thereto, shall be used, and the elevation of the projecting arm shall not exceed 15 degrees, viz., so as to throw the pigeons from four to fifteen feet in vertical height above the level of the trap bottom. In trap No. 3, the third notch, or a velocity equivalent thereto, shall be used, with the same elevation.

RULE 13. *Setting of Traps.*—A straight line shall be drawn from the score, at eighteen yards in the rear, to trap No. 3, and extended to a point not further than seven yards in front of same. Traps Nos. 1 and 5 shall be set to throw the birds across this line, the crossing point being anywhere within the seven yards point in front of trap 3. Trap No. 2 shall throw in a direction left half quartering from the score; trap No. 4 shall throw in a direction right half quartering upon the score; and trap No. 3 shall throw straight-away.

If, after such setting of the traps, the birds, for any reason, take other directions, they shall be considered fair birds.

RULE 14. *Pulling of Traps.*—When the shooter calls "Pull" the trap shall be instantly sprung, or the bird may be refused. If pulled without notice, or more than one bird loosed, the shot may be refused; but, if taken it is to be scored. If the shooter fails to shoot when the trap is properly pulled, it must be scored a lost bird.

RULE 15. *Position of Puller.*—The trap-puller shall stand from four to six feet behind the shooter, and shall use his own discretion in regard to which trap shall be sprung for each shooter, but he shall pull equally and regularly for all shooters.

RULE 16. *Screens, Netting, Trench.*—No screens or netting shall be used; "back stops" may be provided for trappers not to exceed ten yards from the end traps, and not to exceed three feet in height.

But, when the grounds permit, a trench may be dug to shield the trapper, without obstructing the view of the traps from the shooter.

RULE 17. *Double Birds, Trap Setting.*—Doubles shall be thrown from traps Nos. 2 and 3.

Trap No. 3 shall be set at about fifteen degrees elevation; trap No. 2 at about twenty degrees elevation, in double bird shooting; and trap No. 4 when used for shooting off ties in doubles, shall be set at about the latter elevation.

RULE 18. *Ties and Traps for Ties.*—Ties on single birds shall be thrown from traps Nos. 1, 2, and 5.

Ties on double birds from traps Nos. 3 and 4.

ART. IV.—THE GUN.

RULE 19. *Position of Gun.*—The gun shall be held below the arm-pit, until the shooter calls "Pull;" otherwise, if challenged, the shot shall be declared a "lost" bird, whether hit or missed.

RULE 20. *Loading of Gun.*—Charge of powder unlimited; charge of shot not to exceed 1¼ oz., Dixon's standard measure, No. 1106 "dipped" measure. Any shooter using a larger quantity of shot shall forfeit all entrance money and rights in the match, and shall be subject to further action by the management, as provided in the Constitution and By-Laws.

RULE 21. *Handicap of Gun.*—No guns larger than 10 bore shall be allowed. Guns of 12 gauge weighing 8 pounds or under, shall be allowed two yards. Guns of smaller calibre than 12 gauge shall be shot at the same rise as the latter.

ART. V.—THE INANIMATE TARGET OR CLAY PIGEON.

RULE 22. *Broken Birds.*—No clay pigeon shall be retrieved to be examined for shot marks. A clay pigeon, to be scored broken, must be broken so as to be plainly seen in the air; that is a piece must be clearly and perceptibly broken from it in the air by the shot, before it touches the ground.

RULE 23. *Lost Birds.*—A. All clay pigeons not broken in the air as above defined, and not ruled as "no birds," shall be scored lost.

B. When shooting at single clay pigeons, one barrel only shall be loaded; should more than one barrel be loaded, the shot shall be scored lost.

RULE 24. *Imperfect or "No Birds."*—If a clay pigeon be broken by the trap, it shall be optional with the shooter to accept it; if he accepts, the result shall be scored.

RULE 25. *Allowing Another Bird.*—The shooter shall be allowed another clay pigeon under either of the following contingencies:—

A. In single bird shooting, if two or more are sprung instead of one.

B. If the pigeon is sprung before or at any noticeable interval after the shooter calls "Pull."

C. If the pigeon does not fly twenty-eight yards from its trap, passing over a line (imaginary), at a distance of ten yards from the traps, and four feet high at the latter distance. The spirit of this rule is to this effect: that the bird shall attain an elevation of not less than four feet within ten yards from the trap.

D. If the shooter's gun, being properly loaded and cocked, does not go off through any cause whatever, except through the fault of the shooter.

E. If a pigeon is thrown so that to shoot in proper time it would endanger life or property.

But if the shooter, in either of the foregoing contingencies, fires at the pigeon, he is to be deemed as accepting it, and the shot must be scored according to its results.

RULE 26. *Double Birds.*—A. In case one be a fair bird and the other an imperfect or no bird, the shooter shall shoot at a new pair; both birds must be sprung at once, otherwise they shall be " no birds."

B. If a shooter fires both barrels at one bird in succession, they shall be scored lost.

C. In double bird shooting, in case of misfire of either barrel, through no fault of the shooter, he shall shoot at another pair.

ART. VI.—RISES AND TIES.

RULE 27. *The Rise.*—The rise, in championship matches and sweepstakes, where no handicap has been recorded, when ten bore guns are used, shall be eighteen yards in single, and fifteen yards for double clay pigeon shooting. When ties are shot off, the rise shall be increased two yards until the limit of the handicap is reached. See handicap rules.

RULE 28. *Ties.*—Ties shall be shot at singles at three birds each, and at doubles at one pair.

Ties in championship matches shall be shot at five singles (thrown from five traps) and two doubles.

RULE 29. *Time of Shooting Ties.*—All ties shall be shot off on the same grounds, immediately after the match, if they can be concluded before sunset. If they cannot, they shall be concluded on the following day, unless otherwise directed by the judges. This, however, shall not prevent the ties from dividing the prizes by agreement. Should one refuse then the tie must be shot off. Any one of the persons tieing, being absent thirty minutes after the time agreed upon to shoot them off, without permission of the judges, shall forfeit his right to shoot in the tie.

RULE 30. *Extreme Limit Tie.*—When a shooter is to shoot off a tie, who has previously thereto been handicapped to the extreme limit, he and his opponents shall shoot in the tie at the same distance they each occupied when it occurred.

ART. VII.—TEAM SHOOTING.

RULE 31. *What Constitutes a Club.*—The only club which will be recognized by the Association for the purpose of contests, is a club which has been duly organized, with the usual officers, and a *bona-fide* membership of permanent standing, which maintains its organization by stated meetings and practical work. No clubs can be extemporized and admitted solely for the purpose of shooting in contests.

RULE 32. *Age of Clubs and Members.*—Clubs entering teams must be known as regularly organized gun clubs at least one month previous to the tournament; members of entered teams must be in good standing the same length of time, and be endorsed by the President and Secretary of their respective clubs. Shooters belonging to two or more clubs must shoot with their home clubs, and can shoot with one team only.

RULE 33. *Order of Shooting.*—The teams, in team shoots, will be called to the "score" in the order designated by the Executive Committee; said order will be determined by the dates of original entry, teams being allowed to choose accordingly; the members of the team will be called to the "score" in the order designated by their respective captains, each member shooting at five single birds in succession, and then (when all the teams have finished shooting at single birds) the members will, in a similar manner, finish their scores at the double birds.

RULE 34. *What Constitutes a Team.*—In team championship matches, teams of three to five must be residents of the same State, and in twin team championship matches, both must be residents of the same county or parish. Any State or county can enter as many teams as they see fit. In team or club match, other than championships, there shall be no restrictions as to residence of members excepting as stated in the program.

RULE 35. *No Division of First Championship Prize.*—In all championship matches, whether teams or individuals, there shall be no division of prizes or purses among the first scorers or winners of first championship prizes, money or badges, under penalty of expulsion from the Association.

ART. VIII.—PURSES.

RULE 36. *Division of Purses.*—In sweepstake matches, if the number of entries is less than twelve, the net purses shall be divided in two sums, viz., sixty per cent and forty per cent: and if the number of entries is over twelve and less than forty, the net purses shall be divided into three sums, viz., fifty per cent, thirty per cent, and twenty per cent. If the number exceeds forty, the net purses shall be divided into four sums, viz., forty per cent, thirty per cent, twenty per cent and ten per cent.

RULE 37. *Association Percentage.*—In all tournaments conducted by the Association, five per cent shall be first deducted from all purses for the benefit of the Association; clubs shall deduct two per cent, in club matches, should the club so elect.

RULE 38. *Paying for Birds.*—The price of birds shall be extra, excepting in miss-and-out matches, where it shall be deducted from the entrance purse.

RULE 39. *Guaranteed Purse.*—Where a purse is guaranteed by the Association, if the entrance fees collectively exceed the guaranteed purse, all such excess shall accrue to the guarantors, viz., the Association; if less, then the Association shall supply the deficiency. Purses mentioned in the program are not guaranteed, unless especially so stated.

ART. IX.—HANDICAPS.

RULE 40. *No Handicaps for Championships.*—In championship contests there shall be no handicap, except for guns; nor shall winners of such contests in team championships be handicapped on account of such winning.

RULE 41.—*Permanent Handicap.*—There shall be a Permanent Handicap for each shooter in all other than in championship matches. This handicap shall be made by the Executive Committee, who, immediately after each international or interstate tournament, shall classify every participant therein, and assign to him a handicap which may range from fifteen up to, but not exceed, twenty yards, for singles, and three yards less for doubles. Such handicap shall attach to such shooter thereafter (until altered) in every tournament and match in which he shall engage, when he is shooting in any Association sweepstakes; and he must daily begin his shooting at this handicap.

RULE 42. *Temporary Handicap.*—In addition to the permanent handicap there shall be a temporary daily handicap, as follows: If a shooter, having already a Permanent Handicap, shall become a winner in a daily shoot, he shall be handicapped because of such winning, in accordance with the following rule: All winners or dividers of first money shall be handicapped two yards; winners or (dividers) of second money shall be handicapped one yard; maximum handicap, 22 yards. That is to say, if by the scorer's card it appears he is a winner or divider of first money, he shall be handicapped two yards, and if second money, one yard. Winners of third money are not to be handicapped for such winning. Upon presenting the scorer's card, which entitles the shooter to payment of his winnings, the executive officer shall, when paying, mark upon the shooter's handicap card the temporary handicap thus made, which shall govern for the remainder of that day. Provided, however, that in no event shall the maximum of the permanent and temporary handicap combined exceed 22 yards for "singles," and three yards less for "doubles." If the shooter still continues to win at his maximum handicap, the other shooters shall step in towards the traps, the same distance that the successful shooter would have otherwise been placed back.

RULE 43. *New Members' Handicap.*—New members, whose shooting is unknown, shall be handicapped for the first time indicated in Rules 21 and 27, though the Chief Executive Officer shall be authorized to change same, at any time during the tournament, after his present match.

RULE 44. *Non-Winners' Match Handicap.*—Winners in sweepstake matches which are open only to non-winners in previous program matches, shall not be handicapped on account of said winnings in the future program matches of the same tournament, but said winners shall be handicapped in all extra matches, whether shot at the main five traps, or at any extra traps which may be in use on the grounds.

RULE 45. *Extra Match Handicap.*—All matches duly announced in the program are termed "Program Matches;" all others "Extra Matches," whether shot at the main five traps, or at any other traps in use on the grounds. Winners in all "Extra Matches" shall be handicapped according to the above rules in all subsequent extra matches only.

ART. X.—CARDS.

RULE 46. *Handicap Cards.*—The Secretary of the Association shall issue to each member a Handicap Card, which shall bear on its face the name of the shooter, the date of issue, and his permanent handicap, and blanks for temporary handicap records and payment of annual dues. The Secretary shall keep a record of all such cards issued. In the absence of the Secretary, the Chief Executive Officer of the Association on the grounds of a shoot, shall issue such card to any member who has not obtained one, and make a duplicate thereof, to be forwarded to the Secretary.

If the permanent handicap is changed by the Executive Committee, the old card shall be surrendered at the time of issuing the new one.

A permanent handicap shall not be changed during a shooting contest.

When a shooter is called to the score, he shall show his Handicap Card to the scorer (who will mark the handicap on the score book), and also to the referee.

Shooters must provide themselves with Handicap Cards before going to the score.

The Chief Executive Officer shall countersign all Handicap Cards issued by the Secretary. At the beginning of a tournament, shooters shall present their cards to the Executive Officer to be countersigned.

RULE 47. *Pigeon Cards.*—The Secretary shall provide the Chief Executive Officer with "Pigeon Cards," which for live pigeons, shall bear the numbers from one to twenty, inclusive, and shall be sold by the Executive Officer for $5; and which, for clay pigeons or other artificial targets, shall be numbered from one to thirty-three inclusive, and shall be sold for $1.50. The same shall bear the signature of the Secretary and the Chief Executive Officer. The scorer will punch these before the pigeons are used. All shooters must provide themselves with their respective cards before going to the score, and unused portions thereof will be redeemed at the rate at which they were issued.

RULE 48. *Winners' Cards.*—At the conclusion of each match, the scorer shall announce the winners, and shall fill out a card containing date, place and number of the match, name of the winner, whether 1st, 2d, or 3d, etc., number of entries, amount of entrance fee, percentage to be d ducted, and sign it as scorer. The winner shall present it to the Executive Officer, who, after adding the Temporary Handicap to his record card, shall thereupon pay the amount stated, and make a record of it in his minute book. A iy complaint as to the amount stated must be made before receiving payme at. These cards must subsequently be transmitted by the Executive Officer to the Secretary.

ART. XI.—PROHIBITIONS AND FINES

RULE 49. *Prohibitions.*—None but members shall shoot in any contest, unless otherwise announced in the special rules by the Executive Committee.

RULE 50. *Wire Cartridges Prohibited.*—Wire cartridges and concentrators are, on the ground of safety, strictly prohibited; also the admixture of dust, grease, oil, or any other substance to the shot.

RULE 51. *Muzzle-Loaders Prohibited.*—On the ground of safety, and for the general convenience of the shooters, muzzle loaders are prohibited.

RULE 52. *Fines.*—A fine of one dollar, to be added to the purses, shall be rigidly exacted for any of the following acts of negligence:—

A. Pointing a gun at any one under any circumstances.

B. Firing off a gun, except when the shooter has been called to shoot, and is at the score.

C. Closing a gun with cartridge in before arriving at the score, or pointing toward the shooter or spectators when in the act of closing it.

D. Quitting the score without extracting a loaded cartridge unfired.

E. Having a loaded gun anywhere on the ground, except when at the score.

RULE 53. *Fines for Boisterous Wrangling.*—Should any contestant attempt to take any undue advantage of a shooter when at the score, in order to cause him to lose a bird, or should any contestant create or participate in any disturbance, or loud, boisterous wrangling during a shoot, he shall be fined not less than $5, or expelled from the Association, in the manner provided for in the Constitution and By-Laws.

RULE 54. *Bribery.*—Any shooter convicted of an attempt to bribe, or in any manner influence the trappers, judges, scorers, referee or pullers, shall be barred from all further contests during the tournament, and shall be expelled from the Association.

ART. XII.—EXECUTIVE COMMITTEE.

RULE 55. *Changing Sweepstakes.*—Through the Chief Executive Officer, the Executive Committee reserve the right to add to, change or omit, any sweepstakes or matches.

RULE 56. *Barring Professional Shooters.*—They reserve the right to bar out, upon request of any two amateur shooters in the, match, any publicly known professional shooter, and also any shooter who is well known to them to be ungentlemanly or disputatious.

RULE 57. *Recognize no Bets.*—They will not recognize bets, nor decide any matters arising from them. Neither shall judges or referees do so.

RULE 58. *Changing Rules.*—Rules announced to govern tournament shall not be changed within thirty days of the date of the tournament; but while a tournament is progressing, rules may be made to govern future tournaments.

RULE 59. *Duties of Chief Executive Officer.*—All entrance moneys shall be held by the Chief Executive Officer representing the Association on the grounds. He shall divide the purses, retaining the percentages. . He shall mark with ink on the handicap card of the winners the date and the temporary handicap for the day, and shall make a record thereof in his daily minute book.

He shall take charge of the score books every night during the tournament.

He shall have authority to employ such subordinates as he may require.

He shall countersign the handicap cards. He shall have authority to change the permanent handicap cards of unknown members.

He shall sell the "Pigeon Cards" and redeem any unused parts thereof.

ART. XIII.—MATCHES PER TELEGRAPH.

RULE 60. Teams or individuals may arrange matches, or the Association may arrange same, to be shot by each at their own respective localities, without coming together, upon complying with the following conditions, viz. :—

The entrance fee shall be sent by mail, to the Secretary of the Association, to reach him before the shooting begins. If the entrance fee is not sent by mail, it may be sent by telegraph one hour before the shooting begins. Any person not a member, who desires to enter, may send by mail or telegraph one hour before the shooting begins, an initiation or member's fee of $5, and the entrance fee besides.

All the rules heretofore stated shall apply equally to such matches. Members shall shoot at their permanent handicaps. Those who have no handicap record, shall shoot at the usual distance, eighteen yards, etc. The result of each score must be telegraphed as the same is made, to the Secretary of the Association. The scores must also be mailed to him the same day, and their accuracy certified to by the President and Secretary of the local club, or by two disinterested and responsible witnesses who saw the shooting, and who are members of the Association.

Ties shall be shot off, under these rules, upon the twentieth week day thereafter.

The Executive Committee of the Association will duly announce the result, and decide upon any controverted points. The committee shall have full power to make inquiry as to the accuracy of the scores as reported, and to award the money according as the facts may appear.

ART. XIV.—THE LIVE PIGEON.

The following rules, (in addition to and modification of the preceding rules), apply to live pigeon matches only:—

RULE 61. *The Traps, Rise, Boundary, Challenged Birds.*—All live birds shall be shot from the ground traps, which shall be set five yards apart. Rise twenty-five yards. Use of one barrel only. Boundary unlimited. In case of challenged bird the shooter allowed three minutes to gather it.

RULE 62. *Birds on the Wing.*—In double bird shooting, the bird shall be on the wing when shot at. A bird shot on the ground shall be scored lost. Double birds to be shot at twenty-one yards rise, boundary unlimited; five minutes allowed to gather birds if challenged.

RULE 63. *Ties.*—On single birds, twenty-five yards rise; doubles at twenty-one yards rise.

RULE 64. *Lost Birds, No Bird.*—If a bird is shot at, by any person other than the shooter at the score, the referee shall decide whether it shall be scored lost, or whether he will allow another bird. When traps are sprung, should a bird refuse to fly after a reasonable time, the shooter may call "no bird."

RULE 65. *Gathering Birds.*—It shall be optional with the shooter to gather his own birds or appoint a person to do so for him. In all cases the birds must be gathered by hand, without any forcible means, within three minutes from the time it alights, or it shall be scored a lost bird. All live birds must show some shot marks if challenged.

MAP CASES OF EVERY STYLE AND COMBINATION A SPECIALTY.

SAVES SPACE AND PRESERVES THE MAPS.

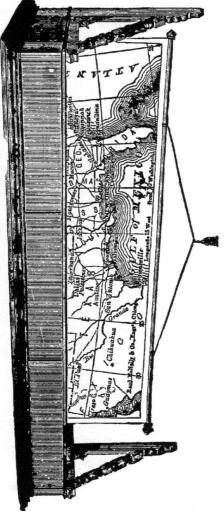

IN BLACK WALNUT, OR CHERRY MAHOGANIZED.

Iside Measurement.

67 x 5x7 inches, to hold seven Spring Rollers			$10 0J
73x15x7	" " " " "	"	12 00
85x15x7	" " " "	"	15 00
103x15x7	" " " "	"	17 00

PRINCIPAL THEATRES.

GRAND OPERA HOUSE, 516 Market St.
ADMISSION: Seats 2,250

Box.....$12.00 and $10.00	Parquette Circle.....$1.00
Parquette.......... 1.00	Balcony ....75 and 50c

GEO. McMANUS, Business Manager.

THE HAGAN, 10th and Pine Sts. Seats 2,250
ADMISSION:

Box, $10; Lodge Box, $6.00	Parquette Circle.....$1.00
Parquette........... 1.00	Balcony..........75 & 50c

HAVLIN & HAGAN, Managers.

OLYMPIC, 107 South Broadway. Seats 2,409
ADMISSION:

Boxes $10.00	Parquette Circle.....$1.00
Parquette.......... 1.00	Balcony........75 and 50c

PAT SHORT, Manager.

POPE'S, 9th and Olive Sts. Seats 2,300
ADMISSION:

Boxes.............$10.00	Parquette Circle..75 & 50c
Parquette........... 75c	Balcony..........25 & 35c

HAVLIN & HAGAN, Managers.

HAVLIN'S, 6th and Walnut Sts. Seats 2,200
ADMISSION:

Box	Parquette Circle..75 & 50c
Parquette.......... 75c	Balcony......... 35 & 25c

J. H. HAVLIN, Manager.

STANDARD, 7th and Walnut Sts. Seats 2,250
ADMISSION:

Box.............. $3.00	Parquette Circle.......50c
Parquette.......... 75c	Balcony... ......35 & 25c

ED. BUTLER, Manager.

PICKWICK, 2621 Washington Ave. Seats 1,000

MEMORIAL HALL, 19th and Lucas Place.
ADDINGTON HALL, 17th and Olive Sts.
ESHER'S, 712 St. Charles St.
LAFAYETTE PARK, 1749 Second Carondelet Ave
LONDON, 24 South Fourth Street.
PALACE THEATRE, 620 Elm Street.
URIG'S CAVE, 2600 Washington Avenue.

GENERAL ATLASES OF THE WORLD.

Appleton's Hand Atlas of the United States, just out, containing nice page maps of each State, giving with each map a descriptive history of each State, with late statistics and resources, etc.; in cloth........ .... $1.50

Berhaus' Physical Atlas, 93 colored sheets, several hundred maps, 2 vols., half Russia 55.00

Black's New Atlas of the World. American Edition; very complete.... ....….. 20.00

Bradley's Large Atlas of the World, very complete in detail ....$25.00 and 27.00

Colton's General Atlas of the World, contains 200 maps and plans, and 130 Imperial folio pages of Descriptive, Historical, Geographical and Statistical 20.00

Cram's American Standard Atlas of the World, (subscription) of over 350 pages of Maps and Index, showing all Cities, Towns, Villages, Post offices and Hamlets, giving Banks, Telegraph, Express and Money Order offices, and population, with index for locating all towns. For Railroad and Express officials, banks, business men, libraries, etc. Cloth, $12.50. Half mo. $15.00. Full Russia Gilt Edge... 17.0

Cram's Atlas of the World, (subscription) Universal, Geographical, Astronomical and Historical. Large quarto, 12x14 inches; 375 pages; embossed and title stamped in gold $5 75; half mo. extra cloth.... .... 7 25

Cram's Unrivaled Atlas of the World (subscription), 12x14 in., : 00 pages; cloth. $4.25; half mo............ --...... 5.75

Gray's General Atlas of the World. Large size; half mo............. .... 18 00

Johnson (A. K)Royal Atlas of Modern Geography with special Index to each map. Folio half Russia; gold edge 50.00

Johnson's Handy Royal Atlas of Modern Geography. Imperial, 4to; half mo., 45 maps......... .... 21.00

Mitchell's General Atlas of the World, 107 maps and plans, and a list of Post-offices and Statistical Tables, list price.................. .... 10.00

Rand, McNally & Co.'s Indexed Atlas of the World, (subscription), contains large Scale Maps of every country upon the face of the globe, together with Historical, Statistical and Descriptive Matter, relative to each: Illustrated with Colored Diagrams, (send for Descriptive Circular), half mo., $22.00, Russia, $24 00; full mo..................... 27.00

Rand, McNally & Co.'s New Indexed Atlas of the World. (subscription). Historical and Descriptive, containing Large Scale Maps of every country of the globe, together with Historical and Descriptive Matter relative to each, and giving a ready reference Index; 731 pages; size, 11½x14½ inches; 82 Double Page Maps and 518 pages of Index Matter. (Send for Descriptive Circular.) Cloth, $10.75; half mo., 12.75 full mo............. . ... 16.50

THE
Favorite Route *from* St. Louis.

Solid Vestibuled Trains,
TO
Chicago, Toledo, Detroit,

WITH THROUGH SLEEPING CARS VIA NIAGARA FALLS TO Grand Central Station, New York,

AND TO **BOSTON** THROUGH THE HOOSAC TUNNEL.

PALACE DINING CARS
ON CHICAGO, NEW YORK AND BOSTON TRAINS.

Pullman Buffet Sleeping Cars,
TO
**KANSAS CITY, COUNCIL BLUFFS, OMAHA,
DENVER, SALT LAKE, SAN FRANCISCO,
DES MOINES, ST. PAUL, AND
MINNEAPOLIS**
WITHOUT CHANGE.

Palace Reclining Chair Cars, Seats Free,
ON ALL THROUGH TRAINS.

ST. LOUIS TICKET OFFICES:
S. E. Cor. Broadway and Olive Street and Union Depot.

CPSIA information can be obtained
at www.ICGtesting.com
Printed in the USA
LVHW011529250723
753313LV00004B/574